LA CONDOTTIERA

Father Virgil Gheorghiu at his home in Paris.

La Condottiera

VIRGIL GHEORGHIU

Translation & Introduction by
Inez Fitzgerald Storck

Afterword by
Thierry Gillybœuf

AROUCA
PRESS

Original French edition published
by Plon (Paris) in 1967.

Kind permission granted for
this first English edition
by Thierry Gillybœuf, the literary
heir for Virgil Gheorghiu's works.

Photo for the frontpiece courtesy
of Thierry Gillybœuf.

ISBN: 978-1-990685-21-7 (pbk)
ISBN: 978-1-990685-22-4 (hardcover)

Arouca Press
PO Box 55003
Bridgeport PO
Waterloo, ON N2J 3G0
Canada
www.aroucapress.com
Send inquiries to info@aroucapress.com

Cover image taken from a photo of
Țetcu Mircea Rareș in Biserica de lemn
„Înălțarea Domnului" din Bica (România)
Courtesy of Wikimedia Commons

To Colette and Jean-Pierre Rudin
V.G.

For Stephanie.
I.F.S.

"It is for liberty that Christ freed us."
— Galatians 5:1

CONTENTS

INTRODUCTION
Inez Fitzgerald Storck

"IT WAS A SUNDAY THEN, AFTER THE divine liturgy. I looked at the people of the village leaving the church....Everyone seemed to be transfigured, despoiled of all earthly occupations, sanctified.... I knew why all their faces were beautiful and their eyes luminous.... After the divine liturgy all the men and all the women of the village were theophores, that is, bearers of God....people who carried within them the dazzling light of God. Their flesh was deified, without weight or volume, transfigured by the light of the divine Spirit."

I came across this passage from Virgil Gheorghiu's *De la vingt-cinquième heure* à *l'heure éternelle* (From the Twenty-Fifth Hour to the Eternal Hour) quoted in Cardinal Robert Sarah's *The Day Is Now Far Spent* (*Le soir approche et déjà le jour baisse*). Who was this Romanian writer, praised by the cardinal whom I held in such high esteem? I had never heard of him. I lost no time in reading the work cited, an autobiography of his childhood, in which Gheorghiu recounts life in the poor village in the Moldovan region of Romania where his father, a Romanian Orthodox priest, was pastor of a small parish. Totally, sacrificially, devoted to his flock, he and his family lived a life of penury, but enriched by a faith akin to certainty, with the keen realization that the angels, saints, and, especially, Our Lady, accompanied them in their earthly pilgrimage.

Gheorghiu, born in 1916, came from a long line of priests on both sides of his family, and hoped that he would be ordained too. A lack of funds to provide for his seminary education led him to take the only option for schooling available to a poor student, to attend a military academy on a scholarship. Out of more than two thousand applicants to the most prestigious of these institutions, located in the town of Chisinau (now the capital of Moldova, then part of Romania), fewer than fifty were accepted, among them Gheorghiu, who after a delay was awarded a scholarship. He was one of only a handful of students who persevered through the rigorous course of studies.

After graduation, he deferred his military service, and in 1936 went to Bucharest to devote himself to writing poetry, his most absorbing interest. For one of his works, *Calligraphy on the Snow,* he received an important prize for poetry from the hands of King Carol of Romania himself. While composing a steady stream of poems, Gheorghiu supported himself through work as a journalist, and became known and valued for his highly personal style. For example, he referred to a young woman lawyer in the news because of her success in a noteworthy case as the "Black Tulip," alluding to the color of attorneys' robes worn in court. Soon Gheorghiu's interest in her became more than professional, and after a short courtship he married Ecaterina Burbea in July of 1939. A month later World War II broke out.

Gheorghiu was called up for military service, eventually sent to work as a war reporter, covering the resistance of the Romanian army to the Soviets, and was later assigned to a military news office in Bucharest as an announcer. But the Germans had occupied Romania in 1940, and General Ion Antonescu, premier turned dictator, imposed the antisemitic policies of the Nazis. Since Gheorghiu's wife's mother was Jewish, he lost his press credentials.

Another career presented itself when through the intervention of a former newspaper colleague who had assumed the directorship of cultural affairs at the

Ministry for Foreign Affairs, Gheorghiu was named cultural attaché at the embassy in Zagreb, Croatia, then under fascist control and a dangerous post, with much of the activity of the antifascist resistance taking place in the capitol. Few countries other than Romania had embassies there. Gheorghiu's duties were largely limited to transmitting to Bucharest information gleaned from official and clandestine radio broadcasts. When on August 23, 1944 the Soviets entered Romania as occupiers, Gheorghiu and his wife fled to the West, seeking political asylum. Yet he was arrested by American authorities in Germany due to his service as a diplomat in a fascist regime. The Gheorghius were imprisoned by the Americans in Germany between 1945 and 1947. When they were freed, Gheorghiu studied theology in Heidelberg, supplementing the philosophy courses he had managed to fit into his schedule in Bucharest. During his years in Germany, he wrote *The Twenty-Fifth Hour*, a novel that became an international bestseller, translated into more than thirty languages. In 1967 it was made into a movie starring Anthony Quinn and Virna Lisi. The novel reflects the suffering of Gheorghiu and his people under both the Nazis and Soviets, and satirizes the dehumanizing mechanization of the Western world.

In 1948 the Gheorghius slipped across the French border illegally, after many unsuccessful attempts, and obtained asylum in France. Unfairly accused of antisemitism, Gheorghiu spent a short time in Argentina, then returned to France where he lived the rest of his life, except for trips to other countries, composing primarily works of fiction in Romanian. In 1963 he was ordained a Romanian Orthodox priest in Paris. He considered that with the imposition of hands at his ordination, he had received the gift of a more sure style in French, and then wrote his later novels and other works in that language.

Gheorghiu's literary output, poetry, war reportage, novels, and biographies, totals over thirty-five volumes. He learned Arabic, and went to Saudi Arabia to do research for his *Life of Mohammed*, told from the point of view of a believing Muslim, but permitting a different assessment. Other biographies include those of St. John Chrysostom, the youth of Martin Luther, and the Patriarch Athenagoras I of Constantinople (1886–1972).

Gheorghiu's many novels have been criticized for their strange plots. Yet his intent is to satirize, to exaggerate in order to heighten impressions, and to make use of surrealism and expressionism to depict various aspects of human suffering. For example, *La Seconde Chance*, referring to a second chance for happiness sought by refugees from the Nazis and Soviets, portrays in the lives of the many characters one tragedy after another, such as the death of a child, suicide of a spouse, impossible work conditions abroad, and persecution for those daring to remain in or return to Romania. It encapsulates and magnifies the suffering of Gheorghiu and his wife after fleeing from the Soviets.

Common themes in Gheorghiu's work are the oppression of the Romanians at the hands of waves of occupiers, including Muslims, Phanars, Nazis, and Soviets; the deep faith of his people, with the supernatural a pervading element in his opus; cruelty of the fascist and communist totalitarian systems; and the dehumanizing tendencies in the West, particularly of the United States, which he sees as given over to a machine-like, sensate culture. He bitterly laments the wholesale handing over of Eastern European countries, including Romania, to the Soviets after World War II. Gheorghiu's last work, his *Mémoires*, was well received, and recounts his childhood, schooling, years in Bucharest, war experience, and time in Croatia prior to his flight to the West. The volume is dedicated to

"the Black Tulip." A further volume of his memoirs
was published posthumously, covering the four years
from his and his wife's departure from Croatia to their
arrival in France, replete with hair-raising adventures.
All his books were banned in communist Romania.

In 1966 Gheorghiu received the Cross of the Romanian Patriarchate from the hands of the Romanian
Patriarch Justinian in Paris for his literary works and
ecclesial activities. The Orthodox Patriarch Athenagoras
also awarded him a cross. These were truly singular
distinctions. After nearly thirty years in the priesthood
and around sixty as a prolific writer, Gheorghiu died
in 1992.

La Condottiera, one of Gheorghiu's first works in
French, starts out as a murder mystery, with the killing
of the miller Nicholas Akathist. Outside of the two
children who discover his body, still warm, the only
person known to be in the village at the time of the
crime was Father Theophorus Akathist, village priest
and brother of the miller. The suspense evoked by the
murder and the subsequent arrest of Father Theophorus
continues until almost the last page.

Woven into the narrative are descriptions of the
brutality of the Soviet invaders and their Romanian
collaborators, and the perennial suffering of the Romanian people. Their penury is exemplified by the childhood and youth of the two Akathist brothers. Later in
the novel, Gheorghiu satirizes the American military
establishment in post-World War II Germany, and the
primacy of moneymaking for Americans, influencing
even their altruistic activities.

The novel is in part a hymn to la Condottiera, the
Mother of God, who watches over her people and
intervenes in their lives, sometimes dramatically. This
appears in hyperbolic fashion in the fantastical account
that the poet Ovid Panteleimon gives of the discovery

of the Americas. He does this to encourage confidence in the intercessory power of Mary. She is, above all, the protectress, the guide, the condottiera of the poor, down-trodden people of Romania, and of the whole earth.

Gheorghiu's style encompasses surrealism, e.g. in the aforementioned story about Columbus's discovery of the Americas, and in the sensation a woman has, when she is the object of lust, of snails and snakes crawling up her skin; expressionism, as in the description of Mavid Zeng, dealer in animal carcasses (later one of the chief communist collaborators), pregnant women falling ill from his stench as he passes by; lyricism, in the poetic description of stars lighting up to rhyme with the candles which the villagers place around the body of the dead miller, among many other poetic passages; and satire, e.g. in the depiction of the American Colonel Goldwin and his focus on pecuniary interests. The vision of a poet permeates the novel, transforming what would be mundane narratives into poetry.

Gheorghiu's account of the killing of the birds in China because they were eating the grain of the people might seem to be an example of surrealism, but this really did happen, the slaughter of the birds, the discovery that they were absolutely necessary to consume insects that destroyed large portions of the harvest, and the repopulation of the birds in China. Gheorghiu transforms this episode into a metaphor of how the communists treated the Romanians, exiling them, imprisoning and assassinating them, until they realized that they needed these people for the functioning of society, and then freed many of them from labor camps.

In depicting the horrors of the regime of the Mus-covites and their collaborators (fellow communists), Gheorghiu relentlessly assails readers with stylized expressions of violence and oppression. A woman is not only raped, but violated repeatedly for days until she faints; when she regains consciousness, the attacks begin again. Mavid Zeng, the merchant of hides, is transformed into an implacable dealer in human flesh, the distasteful operations of his flaying of animal carcasses foreshadowing his torture and assassination of human victims.

The communists apply the death penalty to those who traffic in illegal goods, and who protect those considered enemies of the people, but not to murderers. The fact that one important character believes that those guilty of murder are executed could be attributed to his being unaware of what was going on in the country for a number of years.

As in all his work, Gheorghiu draws on his life experience to depict characters and events. For example, as a boy he planted climbing roses all around his family's partially constructed little house to hide the fact that it was in an unfinished state, due to his father's lack of funds. This transformation of a house to look like it was made of flowers was his first poetic creation, as he recounts in his memoirs, since one of the tasks of the poet is to change ugliness into beauty. In *La Condottiera* the boy Theodore will do the same thing to hide the mean appearance of his father's house. With regard to characters, Gheorghiu's father serves as a model for the physical appearance of Father Theophorus, both seeming to be primarily spiritual beings, lacking in substance, without flesh and bones.

The gentle, fervent piety of believing Romanians contrasts with the dehumanized tactics of the communists. Certain folk beliefs of the peasants give evidence of a deep piety, strictly speaking not forming part of Orthodox doctrine. Confidence in Christ and Our Lady, veneration of recently martyred bishops and priests, and anticipation of eternal life serve as counterfoils to the hatred and violence of the enemy. Gheorghiu refers numerous times to Eastern and Western Church fathers to illustrate reactions and attitudes of some of the characters.

Even though *La Condottiera* covers a wide range of historical scenarios, starting with the age-old domination of the Romanian people under the Muslims and their satraps and so many other oppressors to the distorted outlook of American materialists, the central theme of trust in prayer and the intercession of the Condottiera unifies the book. "Greater is He who is in you than he who is in the world" (1 John 4:4).

✺

I cannot thank my beloved husband Thomas enough for his encouragement, expert editorial assistance, and advice on many aspects of this translation, which he read carefully and commented on in detail. This introduction has also benefitted significantly from his suggestions. I have been incredibly blessed to have him as a constant companion in this undertaking, and during the whole of our earthly pilgrimage together, which he has made a foretaste of heaven.

Many thanks to our multi-talented sons Michael and Gabriel, whose help with computer hardware and software has been indispensable. They have been very generous with their time and expertise.

Special thanks to Iuliu-Marius Morariu, Romanian Orthodox monk, priest, and academic, for his helpful comments on terms associated with Orthodoxy. Any remaining inaccuracies are my responsibility.

May 13, 2022
Feast of Our Lady of Fatima

La Condottiera

I

The Murder of the Miller Nicholas Akathist of Vrancea

IT IS SUNDAY, AUGUST 23, 1964. THE
National Holiday. It is eight o'clock in the evening.
A little before the setting of the sun. The police
chief was notified a half hour ago already that the miller
Nicholas Akathist had been murdered, that his body
was lying in a pool of blood, in the middle of the road,
in front of his mill. Coming closer and closer, the siren
of the police car can be heard, as it passes through the
village of the Akathists and goes up the road parallel
to the river, towards the mill. The jeep of the militia
stops two steps away from the corpse, which is blocking
the road. The first one to go up to the body is Mavid
Zeng, the militia chief of the Vrancea region. He comes
in person to investigate the murder. Never, during his
life, would the good miller have thought that one day
the terrible Mavid Zeng would go out of his way for
him. And now it has happened. As long as the world
has existed, the dead have always been held to be more
important than the living.

Mavid Zeng is a small, puny man about sixty years
old, to whom no recruiters of any army on earth would
ever have given a military uniform. Moreover, he had
been rejected as unfit for service. He had never served
in the military. That doesn't prevent him from appear-
ing today in the impressive uniform of a colonel, with
polished boots, huge epaulets with enormous gold braid
in the style of the Muscovites, his chest covered with

3

decorations. Mavid Zeng is a colonel in the militia. His cap and the collar of his tunic are embroidered in gold with the letters PC. These are the initials of the Party of Collaborators with the occupiers of the country. PC designates the auxiliaries of the Muscovite invader, which occupied the country on August 23, 1944. It is precisely the commemoration of the occupation that the people are celebrating today. Twenty years of occupation.

Colonel Zeng heard of the murder of the miller Nicholas Akathist from the official platform erected at the center of town, from which he watched the parade of the conquered people of Vrancea, that mountainous province located south of Petrodava on the eastern slope of the Carpathians, at the very heart of Romania.

Colonel Mavid Zeng immediately leaves the platform, and arrives at the scene of the crime in dress uniform, with his pistol in a shoulder holster. Mavid Zeng heads toward the corpse without looking at it. Next to the body, there is already a militiaman standing at attention, who delivers a report without being asked.

"The murder was committed barely an hour ago. The victim has been identified. It's the miller Nicholas Akathist, age forty-three, whose residence was at the mill of the Condottiera. Initial findings indicate that he was attacked from behind. As you can see, he was stabbed in the back. Right between the shoulder blades. The victim fell forward onto his stomach, under the force of the blow. And he's still in that position. He must have died instantly. He didn't have time to turn around, to resist, to protect himself. He fell as though struck by lightning."

The militiaman speaking is Zid Caracal. He is in charge of the village of the Akathists. In the herd-like society established by the occupiers, this is an office of great importance. The head of a village has the same power over the residents that a shepherd has over his flock. He is the one who decides what the people eat, where they sleep, when they get up, what clothing they wear, what they should say and think. The Muscovite invaders organize the countries they conquer in the same way they manage their herds on the steppes. They divide the conquered people into flocks, or departments, and put someone in charge of each flock. This official, like a shepherd, distributes food and clothing, and assigns living quarters. The flock of men must, in turn, offer the official all they produce, exactly as sheep must give the shepherd their milk, their wool, their lambs, their skin, their flesh . . .

Unlike Mavid Zeng, the official in charge of the village is a colossus, with an olive complexion and the arms and legs of a gorilla. His pants and jacket are of black leather, and his face is shiny with sweat. Because it is difficult for him to speak. Talking, for Zid Caracal, is as tiring as breaking up stones. This is due to a birth defect. He was born with an overly long and thick tongue. His tongue is huge, like that of an ox. There is no room for his gigantic tongue in his mouth, and so he must make a great muscular effort to form words. People say that at night when he sleeps, Caracal has to keep his mouth open, his tongue leaving its cage and hanging over his lips like a dog's tongue when it is too hot. But this is not the only thing that he has in common with dogs. Zid Caracal also has the disposition of a vicious dog. His only pleasure in life is doing evil, in seeing people suffer physically. As dogs like to bite and tear flesh apart.

"Your Comradeship, I call to your attention that although a man has died — an act obviously committed by another man — in the village of the Akathists, there was no one there at the time of the crime. Absolutely no one. I wonder then, Your Comradeship, who could have killed the miller lying here, since there was no one here to do it. Because it is the action of a man. It was not a ghost who ran the knife into the miller's back. Now, all men were at the assembly, the parade. They had left, under my surveillance, at daybreak. I counted them and took a roll call twice, before forming them into a column for the march, preceded by flags and signs. No resident has come back yet from the parade. The murder was discovered by these two children, who ran up to the Castel Vaca right away to alert the sentinels.... That is all I have to report at present to Your Exalted Comradeship."

Zid Caracal calls his boss "Your Comradeship." Exactly as in other times one addressed his superior as "Your Highness" or "Your Eminence." After August 23, 1944, the day the Muscovite invaders occupied the country, they set up a new society of a herd-like nature. The people, despoiled of all their property, were organized into herds, each with a head official in uniform and armed. In this society where men were organized like animals, polite titles like Mr., Mrs., and Miss were abolished. Everyone was obliged to speak to each other familiarly, referring to each other as "comrade." From the beginning, people were ill at ease, because if cows can refer to each other familiarly as "comrade cow," they find it difficult to call their cowherds "comrade." It was plain as day that they were not comrades. It was no longer a difference of class or rank, but a difference of species, as exists between a cow and a cowherd. The collaborators of the occupation possessed everything, including the power of life and death over the human herd they commanded. The people deemed it acceptable to call the collaborators not "comrade," without a doubt absurd, but "Your Comradeship." Always in the third person. Like "Your Highness." Zid Caracal, even though he was a militiaman and could call his boss "comrade," prefers, due to his servility, to call him "Your Comradeship," like the herd of citizens.

"What children are you talking about?" Mavid Zeng asks. But, looking around, he sees two children actually there. There is a boy about eight years old and a little girl, younger. Their clothes, made of hemp, are very dirty. Their hair is disheveled, their faces are spattered with mud. The two children, who have never washed or had their hair cut, are standing at the edge of the road near the corpse, in fright.

"It's you who found the body?"

The blue eyes of the militia chief of the Vrancea region flash with anger. Zeng shouts, "The time you found the body indicates that you were in the village instead of at the grand parade of the people."

Suddenly the problem of the murder of the miller Akathist becomes a matter of secondary importance. The real crime now is the crime of the children who didn't participate in the National Holiday of August 23, and who have now been found out. Mavid Zeng turns his back to the corpse and speaks to the children in a menacing tone.

"The August 23 holiday, the glorious day when the victorious forces of Muscovites came to our soil, this day, do you understand?" No one, no human creature, has the right to abstain from participating in the great rejoicing of the people and the assemblies demonstrating sentiments of fellowship with the Muscovites.... It is the National Holiday of the people. For that reason, the people are present. Anyone who refrains from crying out for joy is an enemy of the people. Residents who cannot walk yet because they're too small all participate in the collective festivities, from the arms of their mothers or nurses. The old, the infirm, the crippled and sick take part in the procession, pushed in their wheelchairs or carried on stretchers by their attendants or relatives.

But everyone, absolutely everyone, participates in the procession, in the parade of August 23....

Because of his unfamiliar accent, the voice of the militia chief, of the bloodthirsty Mavid Zeng, who has terrorized the land of Vrancea for twenty years, seems even more threatening.

Before the two children have time to open their mouths to reply, Mavid Zeng shouts, "Give me an answer right away, without dodging my question. Why were you absent from the national assembly? What are your names?"

"My name is Sava Trifan, Your Exalted Comradeship. I'm eight years old. This girl is my sister. Her name is Tinca Trifan. She'll be six years old in the fall, in two months..."

"Why were you absent from the people's parade?"

"We stayed away from the great festivities of this glorious day, Your Comradeship, because my little sister and I have scabies...."

"What's that you're saying?"

"Our presence at the National Holiday was forbidden to my sister and me, Your Exalted Comradeship, so that we wouldn't give scabies to the crowds of people if we were near them."

"Scabies?" cries Mavid Zeng. "You have scabies? Is it possible that there is scabies in the territory of the People's Republic?"

Mavid Zeng is so furious that he steps on the hand of the dead man with his polished boots, grinding the fingers of the cadaver into the dust of the road.

"You have scabies?" Mavid Zeng asks again.

"Yes, Your Exalted Comradeship, we have scabies," the boy answers with a touch of pride. This matter takes on such proportions and such breadth that the boy realizes the inestimable value and importance of his scabies, of his little sister Tinca's scabies. They are proud of this. One is always proud of possessing a thing of value. Their scabies is the major concern of His Exalted Comradeship, the militia chief. Their scabies is more important than even the murder of the miller, whose body has been forgotten, whose hands have been trampled on by the militia chief in his boots, crushing them, without noticing it. Sava and Tinca's scabies is more important than the murder, more important even than the crime of being absent from the celebration of August 23. And that is the apogee in the hierarchy. Because if the murder of a man can, strictly speaking, be pardoned, absence from the August 23 celebration is a capital crime, a mortal sin that can be pardoned by no one, for any reason whatsoever. And now something more important than that has been discovered. A thing that they, Sava and Tinca, have on their skin. For the moment, their scabies is the most important thing in the People's Republic of Vrancea.

"It isn't possible that they have scabies, is it, Comrade Zid? There is no scabies in the People's Republic. They're lying, aren't they?"

"They really do have scabies, Your Comradeship. They aren't lying. I've observed their scabies with my own eyes. And I'm the one who forbade their participation in the glorious festivities, so that they wouldn't transmit their scabies to the masses of people on such a glorious day..."

"I've said that there is no scabies in the People's Republic," cries Mavid Zeng.

"Of course, Your Comradeship, there is no scabies in the People's Republic. Certainly not. It is absurd and inconceivable that we could have scabies here. For that reason, I've come to the conclusion that these two children have been to religious places clandestinely. And I'll prove that these children here picked up scabies at the village church.... At medieval ceremonies. That's the only opportunity to get scabies. Not the People's Republic. I'm sure they went to the church, which is strictly forbidden to those under eighteen. And they have scabies. That's the blatant proof. It's only at church that it can be picked up nowadays. Where religious people are..."

"Show me your hands," Mavid Zeng orders.

The two children, who are still standing barefoot in the weeds at the side of the road, go up to him. Between them and Mavid Zeng lies the body of the murdered miller. The children hold out their little dirty hands, above the corpse, below the eyes of the militia chief.

"Spread out your fingers," Zeng orders.

Sava and Tinca Trifan comply. Their fingers are thin, dirty, like little chicken bones. Between their fingers, where their skin is white and delicate, there are innumerable cuts, like red hairs. The skin between the children's fingers is cut, in every direction, as though by a razor blade. That is scabies. The scabies parasites, once they have penetrated the skin of the poor people affected, make cuts from inside, fine incisions. And then a kind of bleeding red spider web is seen on the skin. That is the clandestine work of the little scabies parasites. They only penetrate the skin of the poor, of little ones, and of the conquered. Where the skin is hardened by wind, sun, and work, the little scabies parasites do not manage to tear it from within. They are there, but cannot be seen. This is exactly like cases of social injustice, oppression, profound discontent, and revolt. These calamities affecting the social body can only be seen in pure, delicate, sensitive white places, like the skin between the fingers, in students, poets, philosophers, priests. To see scabies, you have to look between the fingers. On delicate skin. If you want to see the misfortune of a people, you have to look for poets among student youth. The rest of society is like the hardened skin of the heels, the soles of the feet, the face, on which you never see the scabies that is eating away from within. Never.

"This very evening, take these mangy children away and isolate them," Mavid Zeng orders.

In a clean, materialistic society, like the People's Republic, every infection brought on by exposure to medieval-religious milieus must be immediately cauterized with a red hot iron, suppressed, amputated. With no pity. So that the healthy body of the People's Republic can maintain its vigor.

"They are already isolated from our social body, Your Comradeship," Zid Caracal explains. "It's just because they've been isolated that they didn't participate in the glorious national assembly, with all the children of the people. Two days ago they were handed over to the care of a crippled old woman, Anastasia, who also couldn't participate in the great popular festivities because of her infirmity..."

"There is another person who didn't take part in the parade?" cries Mavid Zeng.

"She's a crippled old woman, Your Exalted Comradeship," explains Zid Caracal. His enormous beefy tongue impedes his speech more and more.

"Crippled, you say? Haven't orders been given that the crippled, sick, and maimed in particular be present, in all the contingents that march before the PC leaders on August 23? They are exactly the ones who are most successful in the people's parades. When they appear in a column in their wheelchairs, pushed by nurses, or lying on stretchers, carried on the shoulders of their caregivers in white coats, crying 'Long live the Party of the Collaborators! Long live the Muscovites! Long live the People's Republic!', the masses are electrified with emotion. That's true enthusiasm. We ourselves, the Party heads, who are given homage as we sit on the platform, and spend most of the day doing nothing but that, we too are truly moved.... The procession of consumptives brought on their hospital beds, who cry out, with what remains of their lungs, 'Long live the People's Republic!', brings tears to our eyes, as we sit on the platform. To hear the dying cry 'Long live the Party...', that's what is most moving."

"That's exactly why old Anastasia wasn't brought to the parade, Your Comradeship. She's a deaf-mute. She wouldn't have been able to cry "Long live the Party" like the other sick people. And from the time she was deprived of a voice to proclaim the glory of our party, I believed that it would be the waste of a stretcher to have her in the parade. I told myself that it's only the mute who will not proclaim our glory. And I thought that the best use I could make of this person, for the National Holiday, was to entrust the care of the two children with scabies to her. By keeping the mangy children away from the people, she participated in the National Holiday from a prophylactic point of view, and contributed to the well-being of the People's Republic..."

"If the children with scabies had been confined in the house of the deaf-mute woman, how could they have walked through the village and come here to discover the body? Did they escape? Why were they going about freely in the village streets, bringing their scabies everywhere? It's a crime to let someone with scabies go for a walk..."

"It's true, Your Comradeship, that they walked through the streets.... If they hadn't, they never would have discovered the body of the miller. But the village was empty. Absolutely devoid of every human creature... There was no one in the village to get scabies..."

"They are a public danger. They have no right to walk about the village. There was no human being in the streets or houses, you're saying?"

"No human being in the whole village. Not one. No one to get scabies. I affirm this."

"And animals, couldn't they have picked up scabies from them?" Mavid Zeng asks. "Animals are also a collective good. Just like humans. They're included in the national inventory too. Why were they walking through the streets to infect animals? Especially on such a glorious day, the National Holiday?"

"We weren't taking a walk, Your Comradeship," cries Tinca Trifan, weeping.

"What were you doing on the street, if you weren't taking a walk?"

"We were going to get the flour that the miller leaves for us at the door to the mill, Your Comradeship. We swear to you that we weren't taking a walk. We just went to get the flour for Mother Anastasia."

"What's this business about flour?" Mavid Zeng asks. His rage is at a fever pitch. He left the stand for officials in the course of the parade, to open in person the investigation of the miller Akathist. Before he has even begun, he finds people in the village who were absent from the great assembly. First the children, under the pretext of scabies. Then the old lady, with her deaf-muteness as an excuse. Boycotting the August 23 festivity is worse than committing a murder. He hears that the children with scabies walk freely through the streets, threatening to infect the human and animal collectivity. Now he finds out about the clandestine traffic in flour.

"You got the flour right from the mill? Flour, which is distributed exclusively at the stores of the people, in the presence of the militia, in exchange for a ration coupon and proof that the recipient works to earn his bread. Any other distribution of flour, outside official channels, is a crime against the people. It's no longer an ordinary crime, like the murder of this man lying at our feet, which is punished with life imprisonment. Illegal dealing in bread is punished with the death penalty. Administratively. Without losing time with judges. Exactly like crimes against the national security of the People's Republic."

"It wasn't a matter of ordinary bread, Your Comradeship. It was flour for the *prosphora*, bread for the oblation..."

"That's even worse, Comrade Zid. Who gave permission to provide flour for religious practices?"

"It's our own flour, Your Comradeship," says Sava Trifan. "We don't ask anyone for it. We make the *prosphora*, for the liturgy, with ears of wheat that we gather ourselves from the streets and fields.... These ears of wheat have been left behind. There's nothing unlawful."

"There's nothing illegal," Zid Caracal confirms. "I've investigated this. The villagers filed a petition, signed by all of them, asking for two hundred fifty grams of white flour each week for religious services. Since there's no provision in the Party's five-year plan for an allotment of flour for superstitious practices, we refused the request."

"If they want to use their bread ration for magical rites, instead of eating it, no one is preventing them. But don't let them ask the Party for flour..."

"They don't want to use our flour at church. They hold that the flour of the People's Republic is impure, mixed with corn, barley, and oats. For the bread of the offering, they need pure wheat flour. And because we denied them their request, all those who engage in Christian superstitious practices gather ears of wheat from the streets, from the fields, everywhere, ears of wheat left behind after the harvest. They bring this wheat to the mill, and make their superstitious bread, their *prosphora*. I have my eye on them. I know everything they do. And that's what they do. There's no traffic in grain. The amount of wheat they gather is insignificant."

"Just the same, it's a crime against the people, what they do. Every ear of wheat, all grain, everything the earth produces, belongs collectively to the community and must be deposited in the warehouses of the Party, which then distributes it. Stalks left in the field and streets also belong to the people. Anyone who finds them and gathers them must bring them to the warehouses of the people. Otherwise, he's a thief. And a thief is a criminal. Our comrades in China and Albania began the execution of the first five-year plan by putting to death and exterminating all the birds flying in the skies of the People's Republics of China and Albania. This was because the birds steal grains of wheat, corn, and rice which belong to men. Our comrades kill birds because they are thieves. No one can steal the food of the citizens with impunity. I insist, not even the birds of the sky have the right to steal bread from men and animals who work. If the birds fail to understand that, they're killed. All of them. Like criminals and murderers are killed. Every Chinese and Albanian comrade has the right to kill the bird that dares to alight on the soil of the People's Republics to steal grain. It's normal for the crime that's punished with the death penalty, even when it's a matter of birds in the sky, not to be tolerated in superstitious medieval zealots, and in those who observe superstitious religious practices. If fanatics from the church gather stalks left in the streets and fields, they are duty-bound to bring them to the warehouses of the Party. And if they hide them, to use them in dark rites, they'll be punished like the birds of China and Albania, with the death penalty.... That's all I have to say about this. Let's go back now to the corpse lying at our feet. How did you find the body?

Because it's the two of you children with scabies who discovered it?"

"We did," answers Sava Trifan. He's thinking about the poor birds in China and Albania. In the Holy Bible that is read to them each evening, it is said that "God created all the birds" and He saw that it was good.... And He blessed the birds, telling them to multiply on the earth. That was the fifth day of creation. Then, when the misfortune of the flood came, God thought about the little birds too, and He ordered Noah, "Take seven males and seven females of the birds of the sky to preserve their issue."

Sava Trifan has always felt a tender love for God because God, like him, loves birds. In His anger, before the flood, especially because God is a grown-up, He could have forgotten about the birds. Children are the ones who care about little things. Not grown-ups. Well, although God is so great and so important, He thought about the beautiful little birds, and about little things. This is because God is a great poet.

"I asked, how did you discover the body?" cries Mavid Zeng.

"This is how it happened, Your Comradeship. We were walking holding hands, my little sister and I. We were going to get the flour for the *prosphora*. Mother Anastasia told us that Father Theophorus would come to get them this evening. After the parade. When we got close to the mill, my little sister Tinca stopped, and said she didn't want to get the flour any more. She wanted to go back to Mother Anastasia's. She said she was afraid to go with me. I pulled her by the hand and tried to lead her by force. Because we were nearly there. But she sat down on the ground, in the middle of the road. She was crying. Refusing to go any further. I pulled her up. A few meters further, we saw the poor dead miller. Lying in a pool of blood. With the knife stuck in his back. At that moment I understood why my little sister Tinca didn't want to go any further. Girls, like horses, always know things even before they've seen them with their eyes. Girls and animals smell death and misfortune from far off, with their noses, with their skin. As though they had secret eyes and ears. They read the mysteries of life and of destiny. We, the men, need to see things, to touch them first, to make sure they exist. With girls, it's different."

"What did you do when you saw the dead man?"

"First we went up to him. We looked at him closely. The miller was just as you see him now, stretched out in the middle of the road, a little at an angle, with his right cheek pressed against the earth. His earth. Because he loved the road that leads to his mill. He was like a man asleep, his face pressed against the ground. Before touching him, we called to him. By his name. As loud as we could. He didn't answer. We avoided stepping in his blood as we walked. Because there was blood all around his body. And it's a great sin to step on the blood of a man. It's like tramping on his life, his soul, and his flesh. We looked at the miller's face. It was white, like the face of angels. Because he didn't have any more blood. Like angels, who don't have blood either. All his blood had run out. Now you can't see it. Because the earth has completely drunk it. Just as his face isn't white any more. Now it's yellow and purple, like all the faces of the dead. But when we got there, he wasn't completely dead. He was still warm."

"What made you think he wasn't dead?"

"His face didn't have the color of the dead, Your Comradeship. It was white. And then, I tell you, he was warm. My little sister Tinca and I bent over him, and without touching the knife, one after the other we put our ears to his back. We listened. In his chest, there was silence. In his whole body, there was a great silence. Then we understood that he was dead. Tinca also put her ear to his back. And she too failed to hear a heartbeat. No life. In the chest of the miller, there was silence. Death. Poor Nicholas Akathist was certainly deceased ... "

"You were saying that your little sister was afraid to go any further before she had seen the dead man. And when she saw him, she wasn't afraid any more. She even put her ear to the back of the corpse. That doesn't hold water. What's the truth?"

"That's the truth, Your Comradeship. Tinca was terribly afraid before seeing the dead man. On the road, when she sat down on the ground and refused to go further, she saw the danger. She felt it. Without knowing exactly what the danger was. And she was afraid. But, as soon as she saw the dead man, Tinca wasn't afraid at all. You are never afraid of what you see, but of what you're afraid of seeing .... At this point we saw the tragedy, clearly. There was nothing to be afraid of. The calamity was before our eyes."

"When she saw the dead miller, a big knife stuck in his back and lying in a pool of blood, your little sister wasn't afraid. That's what you were saying. But that couldn't be true. You're hiding something. What is the truth?"

"I swear that that's the truth. My little sister stopped being afraid when she saw the dead miller. We were filled with sorrow, sadness, and pity. There was no room for fear in us. Where could fear have found a place, when our hearts were full of sorrow? We crossed ourselves, very devoutly. I said in a loud voice, and Tinca repeated after me, 'May the Lord who created heaven and earth have mercy on the soul of the miller Nicholas Akathist.' Then, we ran to Castel Vaca and we told the sentinel about what we had seen, and how the miller was lying there dead in front of the mill with a big knife in his back.... The sentinel sounded the alarm. Then His Comradeship Zid Caracal brought us here to show him the body."

"Then we're sure that the murder was committed about an hour ago," Mavid Zeng says.

"When I got to the crime scene, the blood of the victim was still warm," Zid Caracal says. "I put my finger in the blood, very close to the knife, in the wound. The blood was warm. It hadn't coagulated. It had just been released from the arteries. The wound even seemed to be still dripping with blood. Because the little drops of blood around the knife seemed fresh like rubies. That proves that the murderer had passed by there some minutes before us. Blood never deceives. The blood indicated the time of the crime, like a chronometer."

"Are you sure, Caracal, that there was no one in the village who could have committed the crime?"

"No one, Your Comradeship. Absolutely no one."

At that very moment, they heard some steps. The steps of a man. They were astonished. They were afraid to look. So there was a man in the village. And this man was walking. Very close to the mill. On the road. He was drawing near. At the same time the policemen and the children all raised their heads. In distress. They stood there with their mouths open. Father Theophorus Akathist, the brother of the murdered miller, was there, in the middle of the road. Just a few steps away. He slowly came toward the people grouped around the corpse of his brother.

When the police and the children looked at him, with amazement in their eyes, the priest stopped. At once. Surprised. His body was immobile. Then, it seemed like he wanted to flee. Disappear. Hide. But the voice of Mavid Zeng ordered, "Come here, monk. Come here."

As the priest drew near, with very small steps betraying fear, terror, and surprise, Mavid Zeng cried out, emphasizing his words, like the words of an oath, "You were telling us, Comrade Caracal, that there was absolutely no one in the village, weren't you?"

Father Theophorus Akathist was now on the scene. Next to the cadaver of his brother. He looked at the dead man, lying in the dust, with his close-fitting white pants, his white shirt stained with blood. With a huge red stain. And in the middle of the red stain, the knife. Stuck into the back of the man. Like an asparagus, like a leek. Right in the middle of his back. Between the shoulders. The priest looked up toward the two children. They were frightened to see him there. Then he turned his gaze toward the policemen. He started to raise his right hand to his forehead, to make the sign of the cross. But the voice of Mavid Zeng cut the gesture short. And the priest dropped his right hand. Without crossing himself.

"Have you been in the village a long time, monk?'

"I've been in the village for about an hour, Your Exalted Comradeship," replies the monk. "For more than an hour." A leaden silence follows, a silence of metal, very heavy, like the silence that descends in prisons, weighing on the prisoners after the guards have twice turned the keys in the locks of the iron doors of the cells. This terrible silence flows down onto the dead man and onto the living who surround him. One would say that even watches have stopped. That sap no longer rose in the tree trunks and blades of grass. That the Ozana River stopped flowing. So grave, overwhelming, unequivocal is the statement of the monk Theophorus Akathist. His words not only close the door of a prison. Heaven also is bolted shut.

The priest himself cannot endure the silence brought on by his words. Neither can he endure the gazes fixed on him. He feels in his flesh, like iron spears, the blue eyes of Mavid Zeng, the black eyes of Zid Caracal, the

little eyes, like those of captive squirrels, of Tinca and
Sava Trifan. All, motionless, look at the monk Akathist
with terror, with astonishment. As though struck by
lightning. One could expect anything. But not that. No.
A priest, a monk, a saint. Because even the enemies
of the Church and the godless acknowledge that the
monk is a saint. And here he, the priest, the monk, the
saint, has killed his brother. He has stabbed his brother
in the back. With the hand of a saint, an ascetic, with
the same hand which touches the body of God on the
altar. The priest has killed. The fact is clear. The dead
man is there. And the criminal as well. He admits, "I
came to the village more than an hour ago. Maybe an
hour and a half, as I don't have a watch..."

The monk speaks to break the silence. A silence like
an immense layer of ice, that covers them all, suffo-
cating them.

"I marched in the parade at eight o'clock, according
to the guidelines. I marched with the consumptives.
When I got to the assembly this morning, they told us
that there weren't enough stretchers to carry the beds of
the consumptives. So they took me out of my column,
to carry the consumptives. All the priests marched with
the consumptives. The parade of the sick ended at five
o'clock. Because they had to be brought back to the
hospital. And to the sanitariums. As for myself and the
other priests, we were ordered to go back home. Before
returning to my church, I came back to the Akathists.
To Mother Anastasia's. To get the *prosphora*. She let me
know that the children had gone to get the flour at the
mill. If I stayed there, she would make me the *prosphora*
for the whole week. After waiting a good while, seeing
that the two children weren't returning, I told myself
that they had decided to play, and had forgotten to go
to the mill. I told Mother Anastasia that I'd go to the
mill myself to get the flour. To my brother's. I knew

where to find it. By the door. And I got here. And I found you here. And misfortune of misfortunes, I see my brother dead.... And Your Exalted Comradeships by him..." The priest dissolves in tears.

"You maintain then that you've been in the village for more than an hour, right?"

"That's the truth, Your Comradeship," the priest replies. "I don't have a watch, but just the same I'm sure that more than an hour went by, perhaps an hour and a half, after I got to the village."

The priest notices the knife in the back of his brother. He had been too overcome with emotion to see it, even though the handle of the knife, made of green wood, springs up like a plant in the back of the dead man. He sees it now, through his tears. He can no longer control himself. He steps forward to kneel beside the dead man and pray.

"You want to look at what happened to your brother up close?" asks Mavid Zeng. He is being ironic. Or rather he wants to be ironic. But he doesn't succeed. Because all this is too serious. There is no place for irony. The gravity of it fills everything. The sky and the earth. Hearts and eyes. Voices and gestures. Everything is grave. People live without thinking about the reckoning of the last judgment, when God will pardon all men for everything, in His divine mercy, but He will not pardon the angels. They are condemned. They will not be judged further. The monk, who lives on earth, angelic like the angels, has no right to unlimited clemency, which benefits people living in the world, lay people. Monks will have the judgment reserved for angels. The crime of a monk is not like the crimes of men. The crime of a monk is similar to the crimes of angels. The angel who sins suddenly becomes a demon, changing his body of gold and light into a black body of darkness and flames.... The last judgment is only for men, not for angels. Monks will certainly appear before the judge, but as St. Theodore the Studite affirms in his *Catecheses*, they will not escape the avenging punishment of God.

The priest monk Theophorus Akathist is more than fifty years old. He doesn't look his age. In spite of his gray hair and beard, one would call him a youth. He is tall, reaching nearly two meters, but is extremely thin, with an ascetic face. His long cassock with its wide sleeves looks like a black flag which floats on his long, dry body, as on the mast of a ship. Still weeping, the monk makes the sign of the cross. He does this in the manner of the monks of the holy mountain Athos, emphatically placing the three fingers of his right hand, joined together, on his forehead, and on his chest, quite a bit higher than his waist. When the priest places his fingers on his right shoulder, he breaks out in a cascade of lamentations. Big tears run down his beard and his cheeks. In spite of his long, sparse beard with its long, silky hair, his ascetic cheeks can be seen, the bones on his face jutting out, almost devoid of flesh, like the bones of a dead man.

"Monk, come here," Mavid Zeng orders. "Save your tears and laments for later. You'll have all the time you need. Now you have to answer some questions. Do you see your dead brother lying at your feet?"

The monk nods in the affirmative. He looks at his brother Nicholas at his feet, lying in the dust of the road, in his blood. The red stain on his shirt is like a big rose with its petals fallen off and scattered.

"Your brother the miller was murdered less than an hour ago. Are you paying attention?"

"I'm listening to you, Your Exalted Comradeship, I'm listening."

"Someone stuck a knife into the back of your brother, as you can see. With force. This is a murder committed by an adult. You agree that this is the work of an adult,

don't you? One can't think otherwise. The blade of
the knife penetrated a good ten centimeters into your
brother's back. The murderer had the strength of an
adult. Of a man. I'm glad you agree with us up to this
point. I hope we'll continue to be in agreement with
what comes next. Listen hard: we know with certainty
that there was no man in the village. You understand?
Not one. Absolutely none. Starting at daybreak, every-
body left the village for the National Holiday. So there
was no man in the village to commit this monstrous
murder. And right at the moment when we asked
ourselves who could have killed your brother, because
there was no one was left in the village to do it, you
appear before us. You came without being called. On
your own. And you even affirm that you were in the
village at the time of the crime ... "

"I was in the village, at the time of the misfortune ... ",
repeats the priest. "I certainly was. But I was ignorant
of what was going on."

"You were the only man in the village, monk. So
you're the only one who could have committed the
murder of the miller, your brother. Only you. This isn't
a murder, it's fratricide. And what's more, the murderer,
the fratricide, is a monk and a priest ... "

"No, Your Exalted Comradeship .... You can't say
that ... "

"If it wasn't you, then who is the murderer? These
two mangy children? They would have needed a stool
to reach the shoulders of your brother and stick the
knife in .... And even if they had stood on a stool,
they wouldn't have been able to drive the entire blade
into the body of your brother. That requires strength.
That's not a job for children. Unless you hold that they
plunged the knife into his back using a hammer, like
one drives a nail into the wall .... You can't maintain
that. That's irresponsible .... The paralytic is left, the

deaf-mute, old Anastasia. They say she never left her yard. You don't mean to tell us that the paralytic left where she was and came here to kill your brother? No? And it's just as well you don't say that. Besides the two children with scabies and the paralyzed woman, there was no one in the village. Except you. So you're the one who did the deed. It's you who killed your brother."

Mavid Zeng looks at his watch. He has to go back to the platform for officials, erected in the center of town, to review the torch-lit parade of all the conquered people of Vrancea, who will cry out all night, bearing torches, about how happy they are to be invaded and occupied by the hordes of Muscovites who came from the east.... And about how beautiful this day, August 23, is for them, when they lost their liberty.... And all night the people of Vrancea will carry resin torches, shouting that they love the Muscovite occupiers, that they love their executioners, the collaborators and auxiliaries of the invader, that they adore their tyrants and that they're the happiest men in the world, ever since they lost their liberty.... Anyone who doesn't shout all that is guilty of a crime against the security of the State.... And they all shout. And the mountains of Vrancea, which alone are silent, weep with all their springs, flooding the valleys with tears...

"The murder of the miller is a matter practically settled," Mavid Zeng says. "We have the murderer. He will give us a complete confession. Comrade Caracal, I'm going back to the assembly. For the torch-lit parade. Take the knife and everything there is in the pockets of the victim. Bring all that, with the prisoner, to the Castel Vaca. I'm going to drive you there. And I'll come back later, at night time. Don't forget: tomorrow the children with scabies must disappear from the village ... "

Mavid Zeng is content with himself. He looks at the corpse. He glances at the monk.

"The mystery of the crime has been cleared up in less time than we thought. The murder, which is an abominable fratricide. A nasty fratricide. Perpetrated the day of our National Holiday, August 23. Later we'll see how and why the monk did this. We'll bring to light a dark matter, religious and medieval. With a throwback to mysticism, sorcery, and other practices which no longer have a place in a People's Republic. We are a clean society. Aseptic. And it's good for those dark mystics, those brothers of Rasputin, those heirs of the bloody Middle Ages, to show themselves, so that they can be eliminated as sites of infection. And after their cauterization, we'll have an aseptic republic. Clean, healthy. The Christian Church is an abscess, the source of infection in our social body..." While Mavid Zeng is speaking, Zid Caracal bends over the body. He removes the knife from the back of the miller. The big knife comes out of the flesh of the dead man, like a carrot out of the moist earth. Like a red beet. Caracal puts the murder weapon beside the body. He doesn't need to search the pockets of the dead man. The peasant costume of Vrancea has no pockets. Hooked to the miller's belt is the key to his mill. A big, handsome iron key. Underneath the black leather belt an embroidered handkerchief is found, with the initials of the deceased: N. A., Nicholas Akathist. That's all the miller had on his person, at the last moment of his life. He had neither identification papers nor money. Nothing. Zid Caracal wraps the knife and the key to the mill in the handkerchief, and puts them in the car.

"Should I put handcuffs on him?" Zid Caracal asks, pushing the monk into the back seat of the car.

"It's not necessary," Mavid Zeng replies. He gets into the seat beside the driver. In the back seat, the priest is beside Zid Caracal. The car backs up, then turns and takes the road that goes up toward the Castel Vaca. The prisoner and the weapon will be left in the care of Zid Caracal. Mavid Zeng will leave to take his place at the center of the platform for officials, to review the torch-lit parade . . . .

✺✺✺✺

In front of the mill, in the middle of the road, where he fell dead with the knife in his back, lies the body of the miller. His blood is now almost black. No arrangements have been made for the removal of the body. Corpses are not like National Holidays. Corpses can wait. The children with scabies, in front of the mill, have also been abandoned. Like the corpse. For them, also, the orders for departure and isolation will come later. Tomorrow. Just like for the dead man. Children with scabies are no more important than the dead.

The sun sets in the sky of Vrancea, in a pool of blood, which stains the whole west, like the blood of the miller Akathist which has stained his shirt red, as well as the earth in front of his mill.

"Stay here, next to the body, Tinca," the boy orders his little sister after the police car has disappeared in the direction of the heights of the Castle of the Cow, behind the fir trees. "Stay here," Sava repeats. "I'm going to run to Mother Anastasia's to get the candles and matches. We have to light a candle near the head of the deceased. The poor miller Nicholas. He can't be left without a lighted candle . . . "

"I'm not staying here," cries Tinca. She hangs onto the arm of her brother. She is afraid. Just as she was afraid to go toward the mill on the road where the dead man was found. She clutches her brother's arm, with fingers marked by the sores of scabies. She repeats, "I'm not staying with the dead man all by myself."

"You have to stay, little sister. It's a serious sin to leave a dead man all alone. You have to keep vigil for a dead person, before burying him."

27

Since the invasion of the Muscovites and the establishment of a society like a flock of animals where men
have the status of a herd and have no right to spiritual
practices, because animals have neither a soul nor
religion, it is forbidden for priests to teach catechism
to children. In spite of that, Sava, who is eight, and
Tinca, who is six, and they are orphans, know the rules
of their faith as well as the priest. Their grandmother
is the one who taught them everything. Sava Trifan
is sad about the death of the miller. But less than one
would have expected. This is because their grandmother
showed them the lines from the book of St. Denis where
he deals with death and knows that death is not an
evil. In the *Geronticon,* it is written: "A monk has just
announced to another monk that his father is dead.
'Stop blaspheming,' the monk tells him. 'My father is
immortal.'" Sava, like every Christian, knows that bodies
and souls will be resurrected. Even the pierced flesh of
the miller will rise again. Because bodies which were
submitted to the same yoke as their souls and which
completed the same pilgrimage, which were enlisted
with them, and which fought the same fight with them,
will receive immortality as a recompense for their sorrows, just like their souls. A Christian considers death,
even a violent one, as a victory. Because the battle of
this life is over.

"The miller is in paradise. Now he's next to the
Panagia and the saints.... Why are you afraid of
staying with a saint," asks Sava.

"The miller wasn't a saint..."

"Now he's in paradise. On this very night, the miller
is next to God. Because one who kills a man takes, as
well as his life, all the sins of the victim. And one who
is murdered, like the miller, goes directly to heaven,
because he doesn't have a single sin.... He is pure,
just as he came out of the waters of the baptismal

font. . . . The murderer took all his sins on himself when he took his life . . . "

"I won't stay with the dead man!" little Tinca cries. "I'm afraid."

"You must stay here, little sister. You are *stupid* and *superstitious*," Sava Trifan says, using the word he heard coming from the mouth of the militia chief just a few moments ago. He says, "Why be afraid of the dead? The dead are better than the living. Because the dead can no longer sin. It's true that they can no longer do good, or repent. Unless they're saints. Because the saints continue to do good, even after their death. But the miller wasn't a saint. He's in paradise. The saint is his brother, Father Theophorus."

"He's the one who killed the miller, his brother, and you say he's a saint . . . "

"Be quiet, imbecile, or you'll go to hell. How can you repeat, on the question of saints, the words of men without God, like Zeng and the militia . . . ? You don't know what the militia did to Our Lord? It's because he is holy, like Our Lord, that Father Theophorus has been accused of the crime and will be immolated . . . . But he has not killed."

"No, I'm afraid," Tinca says, hearing that Father Theophorus will be immolated. Like Christ. Now there's the death of the priest to consider. Tinca weeps.

"If you're afraid of the dead, go to the living," Sava says angrily. "Go to Mother Anastasia's. Get a candle or two. They're below the beam of the ceiling, next to the basil and incense. Don't knock anything over. Get the candles and hurry back. And don't forget the matches . . . "

There haven't been any candles for sale for twenty years. Since the invasion and occupation of Vrancea by the Muscovites. They think they can abolish the faith by banning candles. But, along with the theoretical catechism, the children Sava and Tinca have also learned the practical catechism. Mother Anastasia — a word which means "resurrection" — taught them never to throw away wax, when they're given part of a honeycomb to eat. And all the Christian children who eat honey, in all the land of Vrancea, give the priest the small bits of wax that they chew. This wax, chewed by the children of the region, kept and offered by them, is melted and made into candles. And these are the candles that are lighted at the liturgy, at marriages and baptisms, and placed near the heads of the dead. And neither the dead nor the churches have lacked candles.

✺✺✺✺✺

During the hour that followed the investigation of Mavid Zeng and the militia, Nicholas Akathist had a little candle on each side of his head, stuck into the dust near his forehead. They were made of wax chewed by Tinca and Sava Trifan. Rolled by hand, clumsily. But piously. These two candles were very beautiful. So beautiful that the sky above instantaneously lit up two stars above the head of the dead miller, like two rhymes to these little flames.

A half an hour later, returning from the forced parade where they were obligated, amid the bayonets and pistols of the militia, to cry out that they were happy to be occupied by the invaders from the east, tired as they got back and discovered the corpse, all the inhabitants of the Akathist village went to get candles, like those brought by the children with scabies, from below the beams of their houses. And before eating, drinking, or changing clothes, each villager lit a candle placed next to the body of the dead miller. With each lighted candle in the dust of the road, a star lit up in the sky, rhyming with the little earthly light.

And when night fell on the Akathist village, the corpse of the dead miller, Nicholas Akathist, was surrounded by dozens and dozens of candles which burned around his body, like a mandorla, like the halos on icons, not only encircling the head, but the entire body of Christ Pantocrator. And above the dead man in the mandorla, stars were lit up for the man lying dead on the earth in the land of Vrancea.

But not one resident of Vrancea, not even the children, who see everything, noticed the stars lit up in the firmament above the dead man.

Certainly the inhabitants of the village of the Akathists were looking up, this evening as usual. But they weren't looking at the sky. They were looking at the Castel Vaca, the Castle of the Cow, the seat of the Party and of the militia, where they had locked up the Akathist monk, the priest and confessor of the village. A medieval castle, built like a watchtower, like a lookout post, above the region of Vrancea. They knew that up there the priest monk Theophorus Akathist, the brother of the dead man, was imprisoned.

The residents of Vrancea do not dare to think about anything. They keep their eyes fixed on Castel Vaca. They feel a strain in their necks. They look up towards it. And they do not dare to believe anything. Not a thing. Because they are afraid the sky will fall on them, like a ceiling collapsing. Crushing them all. Such a crime is not conceivable. No. It is a Sunday. Because this year, 1964, August 23 falls on a Sunday. The ninth Sunday after Pentecost. No one has officiated at the liturgy. Not anywhere. Because the priests were obligated to take part in the parade. And this Sunday, the militia claims that the priest of the Akathists, their priest, has killed his brother the miller. And no one can bring himself to go to bed. Because such a crime must have an immediate punishment. A terrible one. Like that of Sodom and Gomorrah. Tonight, the sky will fall. The earth will open and engulf the whole land of Vrancea

31

in its depths of fire and sulphur. Because of the crime committed by the holy monk, no one has the heart to look up at the sky. And it's a pity, because the candle-lit chapel, the chapel of the firmament, with all the stars lit up for the murdered man, is more beautiful than the chapel of repose below: the whole cosmos, plunged into mourning, weeps for the murder of the miller Nicholas Akathist. Because the cosmos was created, in six days, especially for man. And if man dies, the cosmos has no reason to exist. This is why it is said that whoever puts a single man to death will give an account as though he had put the whole universe to death. The cosmos without man is a useless creation, in spite of the beauty of its vegetation, minerals and animals.... All its marvels, the moon and sun, days and nights, flowers and trees, seas and mountains, have been created for man. And it is only for the sake of man that all these created things can arrive at their fullness, their divinization. Without man, nothing achieves a state of plenitude. And here a man is dead. One opportunity for plenitude in the cosmos has disappeared. And the cosmos is in mourning. The one whose mission was to return all creation to a state of fullness, by sanctifying it, the man-priest, has killed his brother. People have seen all kinds of crimes and all kinds of sins under the sun. But never has a greater one been seen. And the moon herself has come out this night, above Vrancea, like a widow, like the widow of the cosmos, in mourning of black crepe. Men lying on their beds felt the sin weigh on their chests like a millstone. All were crushed. Nearly breathless. Suffocated. The crime of the holy monk was too heavy to bear.

II

Vespers at the Castel Vaca

A S THE INHABITANTS OF THE VIL-
lage of the Akathists were returning home from
the national celebration and discovered their
dead miller on the road, the monk was at the Castel
Vaca. The militia car had dropped him off there in the
custody of Zid Caracal. The priest prisoner was shut up
in the castle in an empty room, double locked.

Castel Vaca was built as a watchtower, a lookout
post, on the highest summit in the land of Vrancea.
From Castel Vaca the country can be seen below, as
one sees letters in an open book. It is a castle built by
the successive despots of the region, dating from times
immemorial. For despotism and tyranny are as old as
the world. Each time a foreign invasion is unleashed
on the land and occupies it, the new tyrants always
establish themselves at the Castel Vaca. From there,
they have the whole conquered region at their feet,
and keep watch over it day and night, observing it
from each window and from all the terraces. Exactly
as prison guards keep an eye on prisoners from their
watchtowers.

After the departure of the Turks, who occupied the
castle of the cow, the Castel Vaca, which they called
the seraglio, the Phanariot despots moved in. The
good-dayers, they were called, because the only word
they exchanged with the people of the conquered country during their century-long stay was "good day."

These were the people chosen from among the international riffraff of the Levant and Phanar. Adventurers of the worst kind, who after taking possession of

33

the country, went to Paris for a prolonged stay in the nightclubs there. When they settled in the Carpathians, they decided to introduce a Parisian ambiance at Castel Vaca. First they trimmed the trees, cutting off branches, as they had seen done in the parks of the chateaus of the Loire. With their clipped branches, the vigorous trees of the Carpathians had the pathetic look of convicts whose heads had been shaved. The good-dayer satraps then laid out French-style gardens all around the Castel Vaca. Like childish designs on the graph paper of arithmetic notebooks. The eye looked in vain for a nook of shade, of mystery, of poetry. There was nothing but lines and angles. The geometric pools of water, like splotches on the landscape, though called ponds, were so sad that even the frogs disdained their stagnant water. As for the architecture, the renovations were even more unfortunate. They decided to put gold molding on the ceilings and walls of all the rooms of the castle, in the style of the chateaus of France. They lacked French materials.... A master mason of the country informed the good-dayer despots that he could fashion the moldings by mixing the clay from the Vrancea region with bovine hide. Some attempts were made. The mortar reinforced with cow hairs was easy to mold and, once dry, was as solid as reinforced concrete. Instead of iron wire, generally used for large-scale projects, they put cow hair in the mortar. This resulted in a cow-concrete mixture. They undertook to put molding everywhere, in all the living areas, bedrooms, and galleries of the Castel Vaca. But the cowhide quickly ran out, in spite of the big herds the good-dayers owned. They decided to replace it with sheep's wool, with horse hair, with hair from cats and dogs. That did not work out. Dogs and cats were uselessly sheared. The strange material they needed could not be found in stores. So they requisitioned the hide of all the cows, bulls, and calves that existed in the land of Vrancea. The army and police were charged with undertaking the shearing of all bovines. This was one of the saddest times in the land of Vrancea. The sheared cows, shaved like army recruits, like convicts, were hideous. A cow without hair is like a gigantic bat, like an apocalyptic beast. The dogs of the region saw these new animals, so ugly. They hotly pursued them. The cows scared children and disfigured the landscape. Nearly all the cows of Vrancea were bitten by dogs. What is more, the cows no longer looked at each other, and harried each other, not being able to endure the ugliness of their sisters. At the river, they drank with their eyes shut, so as not to see their own bodies in the mirror of the water. They no longer calved nor gave milk. Because sadness dried up their udders and took away the desire to have little ones. In spite of the huge distress experienced by the cows, they continued to shear them and even to shave them. It was a work of the police day and night. Then, it all ended. The castle was decorated with molding made of cow hair. And because all these embellishments were only possible thanks to the cows, it was called the Castel Vaca. The last good-dayer satrap left the castle at the start of the Second World War, in 1941, and settled in the West. The castle was sold for next to nothing. For less than a mouthful of bread. This is because castles are not bought, they are taken by force. And this was the first time in more than a thousand years that the Castel Vaca was sold and not taken as war booty. The one who bought it, paying less for the castle and its annexes than one would give for a pair of oxen, was Mavid Zeng. In spite of the ridiculous amount that he paid the fleeing despot, no one was deceived. Neither the seller nor the buyer. The good-dayer sold a thing that is generally abandoned for nothing. And Mavid

Zeng bought something that cannot be acquired with money. During the entire duration of the war, Mavid Zeng did not live in the castle. He transformed it into a warehouse for merchandise.

This Mavid Zeng, the new proprietor, was the most well-known man in the land of Vrancea. Even so, they didn't know where he came from, or where he lived, if he was married, if he had relatives or not. They knew nothing about him. But they always found him everywhere. He was on all the roads, at all the fairs, in all the villages and towns. Children, even babies, recognized Zeng. With his big felt hat, his ample cloak which he never took off, even on the warmest days, and on his shoulder his staff of dogwood with a roll of animal skins hanging from it. Before seeing him, they sensed his presence, from his odor. Because as soon as a village cow, horse, dog or cat died, the next day, as though drawn by the odor of the dead animal, Mavid Zeng made his appearance. He talked to the owner, asking if the carcass was in his yard or field. He bargained. Then, from a bag hidden under his cape, he took out a set of butcher's tools — knives, axes, shears and saws. They all shone. And while he was making preparations, the villagers, from the smallest to the most serious, even priests, schoolmasters, and police-men, all gathered round the dead animal and Mavid Zeng. As for a big show. Without removing his hat or cape, Zeng began to cut off the hide of the animal, which he skinned with an adroitness never before seen. He never damaged a hide. Even if he got there too late, after a few days of hot weather, and even if the animal was filled with worms, swollen, putrefied, Mavid Zeng bent over the carcass and beginning with the stomach, took off the skin as one takes off a glove. Sometimes the odor was so strong that the spectators witnessing this operation withdrew dozens of meters back, so they wouldn't collapse from suffocation. Mavid Zeng's nostrils seemed to be protected. He kept his nose in the carcass. While he methodically skinned it, the odor suffocated the others. Not him. Pregnant women fell ill at the mere sight of the putrid flesh and worms. Mavid Zeng worked without gloves, his hands deep in the decayed carcass, with no aversion. Ever. Others were afraid to get near the animal when it had died of sickness. Mavid Zeng had no fear of sickness, just as he had no aversion to whatever assailed his eyes and nostrils. He had been immunized. And after skinning the animal, he took out other shiny instruments and scraped the hide with care, slowly, removing bits of flesh, blood, fat, rot and worms. After cleaning the hide, he wiped his face with his hands and contemplated his work. He took out a bull's horn attached to his belt and sprinkled salt on the hide. Then he rolled it up like something of value, tied it up and hung it from his staff, slung over his shoulder, and departed. He made his farewell without a word, touching his fingers to his broad-brimmed hat. He left behind him traces of his work that remained for hours, the stench of the carcass and of the hide that he carried off. There were times when Mavid Zeng found neither hides of oxen nor of horses or cows. Then he contented himself with small hides. And with the same meticulousness, he searched for and skinned dead bodies of dogs, cats and rats. Mavid Zeng offered the most extraordinary show that Vrancea children could attend. They ran ahead of him as soon as he appeared, with his hat, coarse woolen cloak, staff, and odor. They directed him to all the carcasses of cats, dogs and rats that lay at the edge of the road within the village confines. And they were present at the terrible entertainment of the flaying.

People asked themselves all kinds of questions about Mavid Zeng, that puny little man with blue eyes, sparing of words, who lived off carcasses and hides of dead animals. The mystery associated with this stranger was always on their minds. Sometimes he paid for a carcass. And they wondered how he was able to make money out of this. And why he hadn't chosen another line of work. They didn't dare to ask him anything. They looked at him with horror, disgust, astonishment in their eyes, wide open. Mavid Zeng belonged to another universe. He had never been seen to sit down, to eat or drink. He walked all the time. And when he walked with the roll of hides on his shoulder, he looked neither to the right nor to the left nor upwards. He always looked at the ground in front of him. He appeared to be rather sickly. But he was never ill. Because he was always walking. And the sick don't walk day and night, like him. The people would have been glad to know where he lived. As he must have had a home. Then they said he couldn't have a home, because he was on the road day and night. They knew nothing about him. Whether he had a God, and which one. The police often checked his papers. He kept them in his bag with his tools for cutting up carcasses. They were in order. But the people didn't find out anything about him. Not a thing, except that the authorities had nothing to reproach him with. When it was heard in 1941 that Mavid Zeng had bought the Castel Vaca, no one in the land of Vrancea was surprised. Because the good-dayer had found no one to sell it to. He had wanted to offer it to the town of the Akathists, who had been unwilling to pay for the expense of the transaction, as they didn't have such a sum. They knew that Mavid Zeng had picked up the Castle of the Cow the way he picked up cadavers of animals. The castle was a kind of real-estate cadaver. They said that the transfer of the deed was even payed for by the good-dayer seller.

They felt disgust, pity, and horror towards Zeng the flayer. No one would have thought of treating him as a man. And no one treated him as a man. Ever. How could you treat someone like a man who didn't do the work of a man? He did the work of a hyena. Of a rat. His daily bread, the bread that he earned from carcasses, wasn't bread for humans. He belonged rather to vampires, to dragons and creatures who bring fear during nights of nightmares .... After Zeng passed by, the flayer of carcasses and the dealer in dead animals, they spat, made the sign of the cross, and went to wash their hands and faces ...

And the day of August 23, 1944, when the Muscovite hordes invaded and occupied the country, bringing fire and saber everywhere, they saw him going down to the region of Vrancea with the Muscovites, dressed in the uniform of a Muscovite colonel, with decorations and the PC badge, Party of Collaborators, coming with the invaders, Zeng the flayer. Mavid Zeng himself. Just as filthy as before. But in uniform. He moved into the Castel Vaca, where he placed the following notice: "Comrade Mavid Zeng gives this house to serve as the seat of the PC and of the militia." And since he was the PC head and the chief of the militia of the land of Vrancea, he started out by living at the castle. He had given the castle to himself. He set up in the drawing room with gold molding, in the French style, but with cow's hair. He received the people as he boasted of being a war hero and of having aided the Muscovites to conquer Romania. By way of recompense for his betrayal, he was awarded the command of the region of Vrancea. He was of a cruelty never before seen, even in tales. His strong-arm tactics affected everyone. A third of the population was exterminated in the several months that followed the Muscovite invasion. All goods, furniture, and land were confiscated. The inhabitants of Vrancea were sent in convoys, tied together like animals, to forced labor or to slaughterhouse camps.

Always following the orders of Mavid Zeng, the flayer of dead animals, who, by decision of the invaders, became the flayer of human beings. Towns and villages were emptied of their inhabitants. And all that lasted for twenty years. The work of the flayers and killers began August 23, 1944, at the occupation of Romania. And each year, the day of August 23, all work ceases. The inhabitants, the survivors, are assembled like a herd, obliged to march before the collaborators, carrying signs, shouting that they love the invader, the occupier, that they love their executioners, that they are the happiest men in the world, as they are supervised by Mavid Zeng, the flayer, the merchant dealing in hides of dead animals and trafficking in cadavers.

The land of Vrancea has the odor of blood. Especially at the Castel Vaca, the seat of the PC and the militia. The name of Mavid Zeng exudes terror. It's enough to pronounce it to be struck by the sinister odor of cadavers, of dead animals, to which is added the odor of fresh blood, the odor of the victims tortured at the Castle of the Cow.

It is the odor of death, blood, and tears, this stench of decay, flaying, crime and murder that the priest monk Theophorus Akathist smells as he enters the Castel Vaca guarded by Zid Caracal, at the hour of vespers, this evening of August 23, 1964. He lifts up his eyes to heaven. But he sees only the golden molding of the ceiling. He looks at his feet, and sees the exquisite parquet floor, very beautiful, now covered with a thick layer of filth and burned by the cigarette butts of the militiamen. There is a heavy odor of alcohol, tobacco, sweat, blood, and urine. It is apparent that only one time during these twenty years has an effort been made to clean the parquet floor of Castel Vaca. But it was cleaned, like the light wood and latrines of prisons, with boiling water and detergent. And that was the definitive death of the parquet of the Castel Vaca. The castle has become a sort of slaughterhouse, where day and night for twenty years numberless women and men from the land of Vrancea have been killed, under terrible torture. For it is primarily at the Castel Vaca that they are tortured, mutilated, raped, and killed. Castel Vaca is the sinister abatoir of the conquered people of Vrancea. It is here that the survivors are tied together like bovine beasts and sent to work camps. Those who have been led along the path that goes up through the fir trees to Castel Vaca hardly ever return home. Ever. For twenty years the bodies of those who die here have decomposed in the ravine, where they have been thrown by Zid Caracal and the Collaborators of the Muscovites.

Father Theophorus, although a monk and, theoretically, not supposed to be afraid of death or torture or undergoing martyrdom, exactly like his great bishop in heaven, Christ, is seized with a spasm of terror. He is weak. He knows that his bishop, Christ, also had a moment of fear and sorrow, in the garden of Gethsemane. The monk speaks to the Panagia, to all-holy Mary, Mother of God, because he is terribly afraid. He is defenseless. He knows at the same time that his body is very weak. He will never be able to leave the Castel Vaca alive, like very few privileged persons have. Because he, the monk Theophorus Akathist, can be killed by a single blow. He can be killed by a single punch. The monk weeps, because he is terribly afraid.

As fear is washing over him like ice water, the key in the lock of the gilt door turns twice. Zid Caracal enters, snickering. It's obvious that he's drunk.

"I have very good news for you, monk," says Zid Caracal. "I have orders not to ask you any questions and not to lay a finger on you .... His Exalted Comradeship has reserved the pleasure of questioning you to himself."

41

Zid Caracal looks for a chair. But there is no furniture. He leans against the wall. He says, "We're about the same age, Father Akathist." And he breaks out laughing. Showing his big teeth, like the teeth of a horse, shaking his whale-like body, clad entirely in black leather. He keeps making efforts to enunciate, because his thick tongue impedes his speech.

"We're nearly fifty-three years old, both of us, but you'll die before me .... That's why I'm laughing. You killed only once in your life, just one man. And you'll rot and die in the bowels of a work camp. As for myself, I haven't stopped killing for twenty years. I'm good at math, but even so I couldn't say how many men I've sent to the next world. And I get money for killing, and provisions, and decorations. Killing is an art. It's the most difficult of arts. A science. You, you're educated. You've gone to school. In theory you should conduct yourself better than I do, since I have had no schooling. For that reason, I want to ask you: How could you do such a deplorable job? In all my life, I've never ever seen a crime so badly, so terribly executed. You're the worst murderer that there is ... "

Father Theophorus Akathist is stunned. He is standing up. In his big cassock, which is weathered, discolored. He does not grasp what is happening to him. A monk is like a butterfly that's only at home in silence, in recollection, prayer, and solitude. In worldly affairs, he's lost. For this reason, Father Akathist, who took part in the parade all day, amid clamor and shouting, now feels like he's being swept away by a torrent, tossed about before being crushed. He has a thin silky beard that's half black and half white. At the monastery seminary in Vrancea, they used to tell him, "Akathist, you are a man who is not completely embodied." And that is true. He has never had enough of a body. Not enough bones or flesh. His incarnation had begun, but was never finished. His soul isn't completely clothed in flesh and blood. Even his hair, which he keeps long, falling on his shoulders, and his beard are lacking in thickness. In spite of this, his beard rather resembles a cloud of smoke around his chin and part of his face. His cheeks are bony, thin, yellow. His skin is like parchment. His eyes look feverish. His whole person emanates renunciation, solitude, fasting, and asceticism.

"If you wanted to get rid of your brother, to take his wife — understandable, especially with you, who as a monk don't often, or maybe ever, have the opportunity to see naked women up close — I'm saying if you wanted to take his wife and get rid of him, you could have managed it better. You see, I ... "

"I didn't kill my brother," Father Akathist says.

"I'm not the one you have to tell that to. I received orders not to interrogate you. I'm not asking you any questions. I have orders to keep a watch on you, that's all. I'm only mentioning my astonishment. You put your signature all around the crime. You signed dozens of times. And that's what I don't understand. How you could kill someone with so little skill.... You know, even the devil with all his thousands of tricks wouldn't be able to defend you. You're in a real fix.... If you had asked me for advice on how to go about it..."

"I didn't kill my brother," says the monk. "How could I have committed such a deed? I'm a monk, a priest, living in solitude. A man who has renounced all the world has to offer, from the age of ten, when I entered the monastery. No, Your Comradeship, even if you're one of the godless, you can't accuse me of killing my brother.... It's not conceivable. To kill a man, to kill one's own brother, you have to be completely blinded by passion, self-interest, madness, or drunkenness.... Everyone knows, Your Comradeship, that I have no interest in the world. I've never possessed material goods. Even the clothes I wear don't belong to me. I have no passions. What's more, I've tried for more than forty years to root out, like weeds, not only passions of whatever kind, but also the cause of passions.... Because to be a monk means not only giving everything up, but getting rid of passions as well. To be *apatheia*, without any passions. Neither good nor bad. I've never known foolishness or drunkenness. Since the drunkenness that I aspired to, with God as its source, I never succeeded in finding. I haven't yet climbed high enough on the ladder of spiritual perfection to attain to inebriation on God and to divine madness.... How could I have murdered my brother? Nothing binds me to earth..."

"That's what you say.... I myself don't believe you. People are always attached to the earth. Always. But, His Comradeship Mavid Zeng is the one you'll give an explanation to about why you committed this crime. What's obvious, in spite of your drivel, is that you killed your brother. I wouldn't want to be in your place. I've never seen a criminal so lacking in alibis and ways to defend himself..."

Zid Caracal suddenly breaks out in cascades of laughter. "Tomorrow, you'd have to see the faces of people coming to the church and reading on the locked door: 'Closed due to murder.' 'The priest is in prison for stabbing his own brother to death'.... Maybe that's why Comrade Mavid Zeng ordered me not to hurt you. That's the first time he's told me this in twenty years. He always finds that we're not hard enough on prisoners. No sort of harshness is too much in his eyes. When it comes to punishment, he's very demanding. He has never had any pity. For him, prisoners are like the dead beasts that he used to flay.... But with you, he's proceeding differently. Because you've done us a great service. You even deserve a medal for combatting religion. Our anticlerical propaganda has never had an argument to turn people away once for all from the superstitions of priests and the Church, like the one you've provided us with, by killing your brother. We've certainly made use of antireligious publicity, making known cases of priests who have committed theft, fornication, adultery, who have been drunkards .... But no one has given us, in our antireligious campaign, such a fine gift as yours. You killed your brother, sticking a knife into his back to get hold of his wife. How can it still be said that the hands of priests and monks are holy hands?"

"I did not kill my brother," the monk says. And he weeps. Zid Caracal lets him weep, and leaves, locking the door behind him. The Akathist monk starts to recite the *Psalterion.* For it is the hour of vespers. All of a sudden his face lights up. He finds peace. His eyes, his face, his whole body light up. He is innocent. He has not killed his brother. In spite of that, he will be punished for the murder. For the fratricide. But that is just. Because he, the Akathist monk, committed a murder in the past for which he has never been prosecuted or punished. And from the time he wasn't punished for the murder he committed, it became a matter of justice for him to be punished for the one he didn't commit. He calmly continues his prayer. Prepared to undergo all kinds of torture, thinking that he'll endure this for the murder that he actually committed and which went unpunished by human justice .... The monk Theophore Akathist weeps. And he gets ready to endure the sorrow, shame, and death prepared for him.

III

The Other Murder
Committed by the Monk
Theophorus of Vrancea

THE PRIEST MONK THEOPHORUS
Akathist has decided to expiate the death of his
brother. He has not committed this crime. In
spite of the overwhelming evidence brought forward
by the militia. But more than forty years ago, in his
childhood, he committed a terrible crime. He killed a
man. This is not a murder of interest to the justice of
men. It is a murder that he really committed, in spirit.
Not with a knife or revolver. But for a monk, crimes
committed in spirit are just as serious as those committed materially. The soul is the principle of acts. If
the soul isn't pure, no act is pure. If one kills a man
in spirit, it's just as though he had thrust a knife into
his back.

It's in large part due to this murder, perpetrated at
the age of six-and-a-half, that Theophorus Akathist
became a monk. It's because of this crime that he elected
to spend his whole life in a monastery, in penitence
and prayer. And it's also because of this murder that he
will accept punishment for a crime he did not commit.

Of course Zid Caracal, who is an executioner, and
Mavid Zeng, who has always earned his bread from
carcasses and from crime, these people will never
understand the attitude of Father Akathist. No judge
could understand him. But a Christian, who knows
that spirit and matter are equally part of the human
person and that there is no man who is only spirit just

as there is no man who is only matter, will understand him. Because matter and spirit are the inseparable components of man. *Non totus homo sed pars melior hominis anima est, nec totus homo corpus est, sed inferior hominis pars est.* ("The soul is not the whole man, but his better part; nor is the body the whole man, but his lesser part," St. Augustine.) A murder committed with one's arm or with one's spirit is always a murder. Why would the one who kills with his hand be more guilty than the one who kills with his spirit? Father Akathist committed this real murder.

Here are the facts as they transpired:

Father Theophorus Akathist was born here, at the foot of the Castel Vaca, in the beautiful land of Vrancea, in the extensive eastern outskirts of Europe, on the eastern slope of the Carpathians, in Romania. The village of his birth is called the Akathists. Like himself. The name Akathist is from the most beautiful hymn, the most beautiful prayer of the Church. It is called Akathist because when it is chanted, one must remain standing. *A-Kathist* means, in Greek, Not Seated.

But the name of the village of Vrancea has nothing to do with the religious hymn. It has its origin elsewhere.

The village of the priest monk is called the Akathists, the Not Seated, the Always Standing, because it is made up solely of people without land, of day workers who rent out their labor. They are people who spend their whole existence standing, ready to sign up with an employer and follow him. Not Seated, that's the position proper to the poor. To servants. To the disinherited and the proletariat. The poor always remain standing. It's the rich who are seated. In all the lands belonging to the Castel Vaca, the village inhabitants were the "Not Seated" all their lives. They earned their bread as farm hands, laborers in the field, seasonal workers. It's on account of their condition of poverty that these people of the village were called the Akathists, the Not Seated. They were standing up not because they were always in prayer, but quite simply because they were the proletariat.

The family of the monk Theophorus Akathist was the poorest of the poor Not Seated. And so it bore the name Not Seated twice, once from the village, and a second time because it was their family name. This family deserved the double name of the poor.

The Not Seated of Vrancea, belonging to the proletariat, were not only always standing up, but were also always walking somewhere. In the spring, right after the snow melted, men took up their bundles and went down to the plains on foot, where they were hired as farm workers for the whole summer. In the fall, after the harvest, they picked up their bundles again and went back up to their village. They stayed there a short while. Not long enough to have the time to sit down, because with the first snowflakes they picked up their bundles again and went up to the heights where they cut down trees all winter. Until the snow melted, when they took up their bundles once again and went down to their village where they didn't stay long enough to sit down. For they had to take up their bundles again and go down to the fertile plains for their summer work.

That was the life of the Not Seated, of the Akathists. No name could have suited them better than the one they bore.

An oak tree that fell on the father of the Akathist monk when he was cutting down trees crushed his right leg, some ribs, and his left arm. He was crippled. He was an Akathist, a Not Seated, who wasn't able to be standing up. Or to walk. For a man who during his whole life had to stand up, this was a terrible drama, to be forced to sit down. How could he stand up now, how could he still be an Akathist, when he had an injured leg?

In the village, there wasn't any work for men. There was no land to cultivate. The climate was harsh. And even if there had been work of some sort, who would have hired a cripple?

The priest in the village of the Not Seated, Father Agathon, thought that from the time the poor disabled man couldn't be of any use to the living, he could be of some help to the dead. The dead are less demanding than the living. In the village of the Not Seated, people died a lot. The poor provided death with three times more clients than the rich. First of all there were newborn babies. Only two out of ten in the village survived. And of these two out of ten lived to the age of reason. Then adolescents died, in a ratio of fifty percent. The death of adults occurred at around the age of forty. So there were a great number of deaths in the village. From the time the inhabitants only had the right to live as Not Seated, the first time they were obligated to sit down, they died. Usually a man crippled by an oak tree falling on him would have to die, because he could no longer stand up. Normally, the Akathist brothers, the monk Theophorus and the miller Nicholas, would have been left orphaned. But Father Agathon, seized with pity for the poor injured man, made him an offer.

"Instead of dying, put yourself at the service of the dead," Father Agathon said to him. "You can't stand up or walk. You'll be forced to die of hunger. You have a wife and two children who will also die of hunger. Come and dig graves. I'm past the age where I can do it myself."

As the only able man in the village, the priest was also the gravedigger. But now he was too old for that hard work. A work which, in the village of the Akathists, could only be carried out by a man. The soil of the cemetery is almost like rock. A hard soil. Women cannot dig graves in that stony soil. In addition, for five months of the year the soil is frozen. And ice is as hard as rock. It's very heavy work, digging the grave of a dead person in the Akathist cemetery. What is more, there are days when two or three graves are needed.

"I'll hire you as *Christiac*," the priest proposed. "Since you're a man who's still young, even if you have only one arm and leg, you'll be able to dig the graves of the dead. With only one arm, you'll just have to work twice as long. That's all. Of course, you'll sweep the church and chant the responses at the liturgy and other services. You'll carry the censer, icons, cross, and banners at all the ceremonies."

"And that will feed my wife, my two sons, and myself?" the crippled man asked.

"That will feed you, from time to time. Not all the time, of course. You'll never have enough to satisfy your hunger, you or your family. The wages of the *Christiac* consist in what you get as alms from the faithful. Then, and this is the important thing, the *Christiac* is invited to all the funeral meals. These meals are where you'll actually eat. Just there."

This isn't a job that is accepted with great joy. But it was the only job available. So the father of the Akathist brothers, crippled, became the *Christiac*, servant of the church. This new activity didn't change his financial situation much. But, just the same, a little. For digging a grave, he got the tattered hat of the deceased or his shirt or some other thing. But, as the dead always have brothers, sisters, and children, the family was always considered first, and most frequently the *Christiac* was forgotten, the one who dug the grave of the departed, who carried the cross and incense and who chanted "eternal memory" beside the priest. The *Christiac* received only an invitation to the funeral meal, where he could eat with members of the family, in memory of the deceased.

Just the same it seemed like life was beginning to smile on the disabled man. But a few months after he was hired as *Christiac*, he had to dig the grave of his own wife, who died suddenly. He was left with the two boys. The little one, Nicholas, was sent to a wet nurse, to the home of a good peasant woman, who after she lost her baby didn't know what to do with her milk, and took the son of the *Christiac* to nurse. Nicholas didn't go back to his father's. He grew up with his wet nurse and adoptive mother.

Theophorus, whose baptismal name was Theodore, remained with his father. And as he suffered terribly from boredom and hunger, alone with his father, he had just one distraction, just one pleasure, asking his father, whenever he came back from a funeral meal, what he had eaten, with a detailed description of the dishes. He asked what each was like, its color and flavor. As the *Christiac* told his famished son what he had eaten, Theodore, who was five years old, licked his lips and sometimes cried with delight. But these scenes broke the father's heart. He couldn't get out of recounting all this. The whole day long his son, whose stomach was empty, made him tell about what he had eaten. To put a stop to all these cruel scenes, the father found a solution. Hunger and love are both of them very inventive and ingenious. So his son would be invited to the funeral meals and eat too, the father never went anywhere without him. He took him to the church and made him sing beside him. He took him to the cemetery and made him dig graves with him, especially when the members of the family of the deceased were present. From the age of six, little Theodore carried the cross at the head of the procession at all the religious ceremonies, he carried the censer, he sang as loud as he could at his father's side, the Alleluia, the *Kyrie Eleison*, the Amen. All the liturgical responses. At the age of six, he chanted the Pater Noster by himself, standing in the middle of the church, which brought tears to the eyes of the faithful, particularly his crippled father. These things accomplished and established, the *Christiac* dared to show up at the funeral meals holding his son and assistant by the hand. No one dared to send him away. Even though all the deceased were poor and every bite of bread mattered. The *Christiac* took his son on his knees during the meal, and shared the soup, pilaf and the *coliva* with him, both of them eating from the same spoon. One mouthful for the son, one for the father. After two or three meals, people in the village were used to seeing the *Christiac* seated at the table with his son always on his knees. It's true that to pay for his share, little Theodore sang before and after the meal, louder and more fervently than the priest or his father, "Grant rest, Lord, to your servant, and bring him to paradise where the choirs of saints and of the righteous shine like the stars. May your servant rest in peace. Eternal memory, eternal memory...."

This made everyone there weep, and the family of the deceased felt tremendous gratitude towards Theodore, who sang with so much fervor for their beloved departed, with the voice of an angel. But in spite of the great number of deaths supplied by the poor in the village of two hundred inhabitants, the funeral meals only fed the *Christiac* and his son once a week, or every ten days, or just once a month.

The cruelest of the seasons in the land of Vrancea is the spring. Just as the poor who live near the seashore draw all their food from the water, the people of Vrancea extracted all their food from the forest. To begin with, there were the mushrooms, of countless varieties. There were mulberries, wild strawberries, cherries, honey from the hives of wild bees, and all kinds of roots and other plants. But in the spring, there was nothing. The earth looked like a bombardment had taken place. Not a root, not a leaf to chew on to forget one's hunger, could be found. Winter provisions had long been exhausted and new harvests were far in the future.

All the Akathist men, all the Not Seated, stayed in the village until the snow melted, since logging had ended. They couldn't go down to the plain, because it was still too soon. No one had anything to eat. They languished during that terrible season which is spring, and suffered terribly. The most fervent prayer of the Akathist people was "Lord, save us from spring." For the spring was crueler than fire, which for them had nothing much to devour with its flames. The spring was crueler than floods, because the rivers had nothing much to carry off from the homes of the poor when they swelled up and overflowed their beds. The spring was crueler than epidemics, because it spared no one, while cholera and the plague killed some of the people and spared others.

The spring of the crime was longer and crueler than the monk had known. That spring had begun very early and kept on. Just when they thought it was coming to an end, snow began to fall. Then the sun came out. But the next night there was frost. People became mad from hunger, from the waiting, and from uncertainty about the weather, which wasn't following the seasons as it should. Then there was the foehn, that vertical wind that strikes from above right at your head and affects those with sensitive nerves. The cruelest thing was not just that this weather wasn't going away, making way for a true spring, but that the illnesses clinging to the sick kept them from recovering, or dying. Spring is the season of death for consumptives, the elderly, the weak.... That spring all the sick were at the point of death. Not one of them could get better or die. For weeks there was no burial, although there were a dozen in the throes of death in the village of the Akathists. Particularly a young consumptive, an apprentice cobbler who, due to his illness and penury, had to leave the town where he was and his apprenticeship to come to his poor parents' home in the village, to die. This young apprentice, eighteen years old, hardly had any lungs left. He had spat them up, down to the last bit of tissue, during the winter. He had been at the point of death for months. Everyone knew that consumptives die in the spring. And the whole village waited for spring so that the young apprentice could be delivered from his suffering. Well, spring, that disastrous spring, came. And the sufferings of the dying man continued. He was the victim most cruelly affected by the weather. For as soon as the sick man was ready to breathe his last, the ice, snow, and winter returned. And he lived on. To continue being tortured.

Another victim of the spring was Theodore Akathist. He could no longer endure the hunger. He ate hay and straw. He ate debris from the crumbling wall, from the earth. And that made him feel worse than he had from hunger. One night, when he woke up from hunger, Theodore begged God to let him eat as soon as possible. For him, to eat meant to be at a funeral meal. So someone in the village would have to die. And Theodore immediately thought of the young apprentice cobbler who had been near death for months, and who no longer had any lungs at all. With his whole being, Theodore ardently wished for the death of the sick man so he could eat at his funeral meal. It was a dreadful thing to wish for the death of a man in order to be able to eat, to want a man to die to fill one's stomach. Though only six-and-a-half years old, Theodore Akathist realized that a criminal desire had taken possession of him. He woke up. He fell on his knees before the icon and asked the Lord for forgiveness.

"I beg you, my God, forgive me. I know how criminal it is to desire the death of my neighbor. But it isn't me. It isn't my heart or my reason that wished for the death of the cobbler. It was only my belly, tortured by hunger. My stomach is empty, tortured by hunger. It knows that I only eat when a man in the village dies. That's why my belly wished for the death of the poor sick man. Lord, my soul and my will and my whole being don't agree with my belly. I beg you to forgive me . . . "

Theodore had hardly finished his prayer when someone knocked at the door. It was the mother of the poor sick cobbler.

"My poor son just died," said the mother, grief-stricken. "He breathed his last a few minutes ago. Go ring the bells for the repose of his soul, *Christiac* . . . . Ring all the bells." The mother tore out her hair and wept . . .

Theodore felt guilty of the cobbler's death. He chanted at the burial ceremony, but at the funeral meal, he did not touch the food. He went to Father Agathon, and begged him to hear his confession.

"I've committed a crime," Theodore said. And he implored, "Hear my confession!"

"What crime have you committed, at your age, poor child?"

"I'll tell you in confession." And Theodore knelt before the altar and the icon of the Lord. He waited for the priest to put his stole, the *Epitrachelion*, on his head and to tell him:

"My brother, do not be ashamed to say why you have come before God and before me, because it is not to me that you make your confession but to God, in whose presence you are . . . " But the priest did not put his stole on the head of the little penitent.

"Theodore, you're too young to make your confession. You haven't reached the age of reason. So you have no sins. To commit a sin, you need discernment, knowledge of what good is and what evil is . . . . Wait a while. Right now you are innocent of all sin because you're too little . . . "

"I have killed a man, Father," Theodore says, crying. "I want to go to confession."

"You killed him by your own hand?"

"No, Father. It's with my stomach that I killed him."

He wept. He explained how he desired the cobbler's death. And how he had died immediately, just when Theodore had wished for his death, to be able to eat at the funeral dinner . . .

Theodore waited for the priest to say, "My son, who have confessed to me, an unworthy priest, I do not have the power to take away your sins in this world: only God can do this. But by virtue of the divine words which after the resurrection were said to the Apostles, 'whose sins you shall forgive, they are forgiven and whose sins you shall retain, they are retained' and trusting in these words, we too say to you: All you have confessed to my humble person, all that you have failed to say whether through ignorance or forgetfulness, whatever it may be, may God forgive you in this world and the next."

Instead of these words, which burn as a purifying fire in the ears, soul, and flesh, Theodore felt the hand of the priest caressing his head. He was crushed by his sin. He was ill. Ready to die. He fainted.

In the course of long weeks, Theodore Akathist kept to his sick bed, hovering between life and death. Then he was cured. The cherry trees, the apricot trees, and the apple trees were all blossoming, as though in bridal gowns. The first thing Theodore found out afterwards was that his father was dying. The old Akathist was feverish. His mind wandered. He was like a shadow. He said to his son, "Theodore, I am leaving this earth. In a short while I'll be dead. Your brother is at the home of his old wet nurse, who is like a mother to him. But you, you're not even seven years old and you're alone, absolutely alone, in the world. For this reason, I've been waiting for you to get better, with my heart in my mouth, so that I could talk to you before I leave."

"I want to be a monk, Father!"

"You can't become a monk. You're six-and-a-half years old. You're too young for anything."

The only thing to be done with a poor child without a mother and close to losing his father was to make a gift of him, to offer him to a rich family. But the Not Seated of the land of Vrancea, if they could have contact with heaven and the angels from time to time, had no, absolutely no, relations with the rich. Theodore could not be offered to the rich, because they were further from the Akathists than the moon and stars. There was only the army and the monastery. If a child was given to the army or monastery, they were obligated to take him. Because they couldn't throw him in the river. So Theodore Akathist was brought to the monastery of Vrancea and offered to the monks. Exactly like a pig, a rooster, a couple of chickens or sacks of corn would be given. The monks received the child. They made him tend the monastery geese in the meadow beside the river. When he was older, he was given the pigs to look after. Then he had to pasture the sheep. After ten years, he got a promotion. He became the cowherd. The next and last step in the hierarchy to which he had access was to take care of the monastery's horses and oxen. For his whole earthly life.

In return for his work, Theodore Akathist was fed and clothed from monastery funds. He ate what was left over from the *Trapeza*, the table of the monks. He would have wanted to attend the religious services, at least from time to time. But his work kept him outside the walls, in the meadows, and he had no opportunity to go to church. Not even at Easter. His place was with the animals, not with the saints. He was an Akathist. A Not Seated. Even at the monastery, he had to keep standing up. Outside.

What was strange was that after entrusting his child to the monks, the dying father regained his health. The Akathist *Christiac* returned to his place among the other Not Seated. He continued to dig the graves of the dead, to chant at all the services, to carry the banners, the cross, and censer at all the religious ceremonies.

Nicholas, Theodore's younger brother, who was now an adolescent, returned to his father's. He was strong and big, and passionately loved to work the earth. Nicholas Akathist was the first to go down to the plains in the spring and the last to return. He loved money and material things. His dream was to become a miller one day. Nicholas Akathist was entirely oriented to this world. He came to the monastery to get his brother and take him back to the village. Theodore refused to return to the world.

As he watched over the geese, sheep, pigs, and cows of the monastery, he never stopped thinking about the cobbler whose death he had wished for so that he could fill his belly. To wish for the death of someone is to commit murder. He went to confession. But confession does not give back lost virginity.

As Saint Nicodemus the Hagiorite explains, "Sin is like a wound, which, heal as it will, leaves a scar; the impress of the sin remains on the soul, and it is impossible for it to be completely effaced in this life. Whoever has stolen one time, or fornicated, or murdered, can never become as innocent and pure as though he had never stolen, fornicated, or murdered . . . " As Basil the Great says in his discourse on virginity, penitence can well remit the sin of a man or woman, but it cannot make a corrupted virgin be as though she had never been corrupted and had remained a virgin.

Now the monk is accused of murder. He is determined to endure the unjust accusation in order to expiate his first crime. He turns toward the east and begins to recite the *Psalterion*. At the Castle of the Cow, the roosters chant at the end of the night. It must be three in the morning. It is the hour of *Orthros*, the morning office.

Just then the swearing and heavy tread of His Exalted Comradeship Mavid Zeng can be heard in the corridor, the chief of the militia coming back from the National Holiday. He asks for the fratricide monk to be brought to him for interrogation on the death of the miller Nicholas Akathist.

IV

The Matter of the Roses

MAVID ZENG IS ALONE WITH THE monk Theophorus Akathist. The old merchant of hides of dead animals, the old flayer of foul-smelling carcasses, who has always astonished the people of Vrancea, because he walked day and night, without even getting tired, still continues to cause astonishment now that he has become the flayer of living beings, multimillionaire and all-powerful head of the region. Zeng is not at all tired. He spent the whole day watching the parade of the defeated, and the torch-lit march back to the village. Then he took part in the banquet of the collaborators. Instead of going to sleep in his silken bed, with blankets embroidered with gold, one of his women beside him, he comes at three o'clock in the morning to investigate the murder of the miller.

"Caracal, leave me alone with the monk," Mavid Zeng orders. "Put guards at the door and go to bed. I want to hear the midnight confession of the fratricide monk."

Zeng opens the file on the priest and says, "You murdered your brother Nicholas so you could get his wife, didn't you? That's your motive for killing him?"

"I did not commit murder."

"I see in your file that you had decided a long time ago to kill your brother. That wasn't a new idea, was it?"

"I never thought of killing my brother."

"And this matter of roses?" asks Mavid Zeng. "You remember, don't you? There are witnesses that you wanted to kill him. Because he pulled out the roses that you planted next to your house."

"No, Your Exalted Comradeship. It's not true that I wanted to kill Nicholas. Not at all. Things happened differently.... You are well aware that we, the Akathist brothers, were the poor of the village. A man in a state of destitution is like a man who finds himself in the middle of a river about to drown. He tries absolutely everything to get out. Extreme poverty is against nature. Man can't endure it for very long, just as he can't keep his head under water. He struggles to get out. My brother and I were very different, in the way we escaped from our penury. We were different in everything. First of all, physically. Nicholas was big, muscular, full of life and strength. I have always been gaunt and thin. He loved material things passionately. I loved the spirit. He grew up at his wet nurse's, close to the earth. I grew up in the monastery, close to heaven. When he was fourteen, he returned home, to our father's. I was no longer there. I was already a monk. He was the master at home. He took the house in hand. He was in charge. He had decided to overcome poverty and become rich. He needed me. So he came to the monastery and said to me:

"'Leave your cassock behind and come back home. Come work at my side. With five arms (because our father had only one) we'll become rich. I'll take care of everything. Come help me. In a few years we'll be able to buy a mill. A fine mill. It will be the mill of the Akathists.'

"'I'm staying at the monastery,' I replied. 'I am consecrated to God.'

"'Exactly because you're consecrated to God, you have to leave the monastery, and come and make money. God is not pleased until men are happy. God wants men to have enough to eat, drink, and to clothe themselves. It's only then that God is content, up in heaven. God wants men, who are made in His image, to succeed

in business, to prosper, and to lead good lives in their
affluence . . . You're well aware that only then is God
pleased . . . . You monks, you make yourselves unhappy
and so you make God Himself unhappy. Because you
can't be happy when your stomach's empty, when
you're forever standing up, and you're in rags. Monks
in starving themselves starve God. When they walk
around in rags, monks dress God in rags. When they
don't keep their bodies warm, they make God cold and
miserable . . . . When a monk sleeps with his head on
a stone instead of a cushion, it's God's head that lies
on a stone . . . . '

"My brother used to say that he, Nicholas, would
make God happy when he had his mill. When he was
a miller. He claimed that all heaven would rejoice on
that day, and that the angels and saints would dance
in the sky, above his mill.

"'It isn't the monk but the miller who serves God
best,' Nicholas said, to convince me to follow him.
He used to say, 'It's the miller who produces flour, for
bread for weddings and baptisms, in the service of life,
and also for funeral meals. God Himself on the table of
the altar comes from the hands of the miller. Because
it's the miller who makes the flour for the bread of
oblation, for the body of Christ . . . The miller works
for heaven and earth, for life and death, for history
and eternity . . . What in the whole cosmos is more
beautiful than flour flowing out of the mill, day and
night, in an inexhaustible white stream that nourishes
and gives joy to the living, makes the dead alive in
memory, and brings God to earth and to men, in the
host and in the chalice?'"

"But you were jealous of your brother, and you refused
to return home to work, didn't you?"

"I didn't leave the monastery. But I accompanied
my brother back to the house. He was absolutely

determined to show me his work, his accomplishments. I went there to visit. To please him. For a few hours. And I was upset to the point of tears at what he had done. If I hadn't been a monk, I wouldn't have been able to control myself. I would have jumped on him and struck him, because he had destroyed all my childhood dreams. He had uprooted them, thrown them into the fire.... With the rose bushes.... Of course, you don't understand. But when I was a boy, from a very young age I had never thrown out the pit of a cherry, peach, or apricot. I carefully kept them. I dried them out, and each spring I planted them. Near the house. My whole childhood, I planted roses, dahlias, basil, lilacs, and all kinds of flowers around our house. More exactly, around the miserable hut that gave us shelter. The house of the Akathists, with trees all around and covered, up to the roof, with creeping roses and all kinds of flowers, was like an immense spray of flowers in the middle of the village. Its misery could no longer be seen. Or its poverty. Everything was covered with flowers and leaves. It was just like with the dead. People cover corpses with flowers and they smell good and are beautiful to look at in their coffins.... And once he had returned to the house, my brother pulled out the rose bushes and flowers. He threw them into the fire. He worked the earth all around the house and planted cabbage, potatoes, carrots, onions, and all kind of vegetables. He showed me his vegetables, telling me that the best soil for a kitchen garden was the land around the house. The soil there is rich.

"'I made a big fire and threw all the flowers into the blaze. You can't live on roses and dahlias. Now there's food on the table for our father. We have something to bite into. We don't have empty stomachs like we did before, looking at the flowers.'"

"Was that when the idea of killing your brother came to you?"

"No, The thought of killing my brother never occurred to me. I was just distressed. Very distressed. And I wept."

"And then?"

"Then I returned to the monastery as quickly as possible."

"You nurtured a deadly hatred for your brother from that day on, and the desire for revenge took hold of you, didn't it? You were waiting for an opportunity. And this opportunity presented itself yesterday evening, August 23, 1964. When both of you were all alone in the village. And you murdered him from behind, like a coward. Sticking the knife into his back."

"I did not kill my brother . . . "

"You had some reasons to do it."

"No, Your Exalted Comradeship. My heart had been wounded. But a monk is formed to endure blows and injuries, and to pardon them. A monk does not hate, does not hold a grudge or ill will. During his whole existence, the monk never stops training to be able to endure insults without getting angry, and to love the one who strikes him . . . "

"You had a second motive, jealousy of your brother. It was the day he met your patron, who abandoned you, and only took care of him. Another offense you were unable to digest. And you hated him."

"I have never had a patron, outside of my Father who is in heaven."

"No lies," says Mavid Zeng. "Who pulled you out of the gutter and sent you to school? That was your protector. Because you were the cowherd and swineherd at the monastery, weren't you?"

"I was the swineherd. And the cowherd. That's true, Your Exalted Comradeship. That's absolutely true. I wasn't yet seven when I entered the monastery. My father was dying. So I wouldn't be left in the street, he offered me to the monks. The monks couldn't turn me down. You never turn down a gift. Even if you don't like it. Even if it's a burden. And I was a burden. At the age of six, I couldn't be a *rasophore*. They couldn't put a cassock on me and make me a monk. So they had me look after the monastery geese. Then when I was older, they entrusted me with the care of the turkeys. Then I watched over their ewes, their sheep. When I was ten, they found that I had matured enough to make me the swineherd. And I remained a swineherd for a while. Then they had me take care of the cows, then the oxen."

"You were the monastery cowherd when Ovid Panteleimon, your patron, noticed you, weren't you?"

"Indeed I was the cowherd. And I was sure I was serving my Father in heaven as I took care of the cows ... "

"That was when that individual told the monks that you deserved better work than a cowherd's?"

"Professor Ovid Panteleimon spent his vacations at the Vrancea monastery. There were a lot of people who came there in the summer. One day, the professor heard me chant. While I kept watch over the animals, I would sing psalms and hymns. At the monastery, I would never go to church, because I had to take care of the animals, even on Sundays. But I knew all the services by heart. I had sung them from childhood, at the village church, with my father. The professor told me that I had a very beautiful voice. He asked me to sing *Axion Estin*, 'It is truly meet and right to praise you, O Theotokos ... ' I sang it to the best of my ability. I loved that hymn, since I knew that an angel had written it with his finger on the wall of a monastery on the Holy Mountain, especially for a monk who didn't know how to pray.... The professor spoke with the hegumen, and asked him to send

65

me to the seminary. They couldn't turn down the request of Professor Panteleimon, who was the friend of metropolitans, bishops, and government ministers. The very next day I was sent to the seminary located within the monastery precinct. I later found out that Ovid Panteleimon is the greatest poet of my country. I asked him for his books. He gave them to me with beautiful inscriptions. And he gave me clothes, shoes, notebooks, and books.... From then on he took a fatherly interest in my schoolwork. My teachers said that I had not only a beautiful voice, but also a good memory and a talent for studies.... The professor was happy that I was held in high regard at the seminary and that I worked hard. The following summer he invited me to dine with him, at the table of the hegumen. During the meal, he said that the name of Akathist was the finest name there was, and that he'd be very happy to have the Akathist name. Then he told the father superior, 'This boy is gifted at art. All artistic gifts come from on high. The creative spirit has the same substance as the tongues of fire that descended from heaven onto the heads of the Apostles, the day of Pentecost. Poets, musicians, philosophers, and all creative spirits are equal to priests, because they are invested by heaven with the gifts of the divine Spirit.'"

"The day your patron met Nicholas, to whom you yourself introduced him, he left you, didn't he? From the day Panteleimon met him he wasn't further concerned with you, and he showered all his attention on him ... And your old jealousy toward your brother was unleashed. You couldn't endure it any longer. You wanted to do away with him. Because you were jealous of him."

"I wasn't the one who needed patronage, but my brother, who was in the world. For a monk, the protection of the Panagia, the all holy Mother of God, is enough . . . . "

"All the same, you were wild with rage against your brother, who had taken away your patron. In the summer when he got to the monastery, he went to the village to see your brother every day, didn't he?"

"I was happy to see him help Nicholas. We, the Akathists, have never been helped by anyone, Your Exalted Comradeship. No one on earth knew us, only God."

"Panteleimon presented your brother with the mill he had dreamed of, didn't he?"

"It's the Mother of God who gave the mill to my brother. It's the Condottiera. The professor helped him to believe, to wish, and to hope. But he isn't the one who gave him the mill."

"The professor was your brother's best man at his wedding, wasn't he? When you saw that, your jealousy, your envy, your hatred knew no bounds. And what made you no longer to be able to contain your venom was the fact that your brother not only had the mill he had dreamed of, and a rich and influential patron, but also that he married a beautiful girl. Because you too were madly in love with the girl your brother married, weren't you? And it was with her help and at her instigation that you killed your own brother, wasn't it?"

"I did not kill my brother."

"The knife found thrust into the back of the corpse belonged to your brother. It was in the mill yesterday evening. On the table. No one went into the house yesterday evening. Except him and his wife. She is your accomplice. She's the one who brought you the knife. And you're the one that plunged it into the back of your brother, when he returned from the National Holiday. You killed him so you could be alone with his wife. Her testimony will prove it. Because tonight we arrested the wife of the victim. She'll be here shortly. You'll be brought face to face. And you'll tell us how both of you designed and executed this monstrous crime."

Mavid Zeng gets up.

He orders the guards to keep watch on the monk prisoner without letting him out of sight for a second.

V

The Akathist Brothers
and La Condottiera

THE MONK THEOPHORUS AKATHIST
is astounded at the accusations heaped on him.
Everything Mavid Zeng the flayer just told him,
as he read the police file, is completely false.

It is true that the Akathist brothers were different
one from the other. The story about the roses he had
planted around the house to hide their poverty is true.
He suffered enormously when his brother pulled up
his flowers in order to plant cabbages and other vegetables. Yet he had never hated his brother on that
account. Just the opposite. He admired him for his
resourcefulness and expertise. Nicholas Akathist loved
the earth. Theophorus loved heaven. One was attached
to matter, the other to spirit. That is all.

The life of Nicholas Akathist took a different turn
from the day the Panagia Condottiera came down to
the land of Vrancea. It was Professor Ovid Panteleimon
who brought her there. It happened like this: Nicholas
Akathist came to the monastery one day. Not to pay his
brother monk a visit. A peasant doesn't waste a summer
day on a visit. Nicholas now possessed a horse and cart.
He had come to buy boards of pine wood. The monastery had a sawmill. By speaking to the monk in charge,
one could buy boards that hadn't been cut right, the
rejects of the sawmill, for a very modest price. Nicholas
loaded his cart to the maximum, paying about half of
what he had reckoned. He had just made a good deal.
He was in a good mood. And because he was in a very

good mood, he remembered that he had a brother at the monastery, and went to see him.

At his brother's, Nicholas met Ovid Panteleimon. It was the first time he had seen him. The professor was a middle-aged man, stout with jet black hair, who talked a lot. He took a liking to Nicholas Akathist from the start. He invited the two Akathist brothers to lunch at the inn outside the monastery enclosure. He told them that he planned to spend a month at the monastery. During the meal, Professor Panteleimon exchanged not a word with the monk. He talked only with Nicholas. With the Akathist who loved the earth.

"My dream, Professor, is to have a mill," Nicholas said.

"A mill?" asked the professor. He burst out laughing. He added, "I myself dream of having all the things I see. I've dreamed of owning a train, a train station, but I've never wanted a mill."

"You have been mistaken," replied Nicholas. "Nothing is worth as much as a mill. To own a mill, here in the region of Vrancea, is to own heaven on earth, Professor."

The professor's face clouded over. It was as though he had all of a sudden left the surface of things, to plunge into their depths. With his poet's intuition, he descended to the deepest strata of the life of his people, as represented by Nicholas. The longing for a mill was the longing for bread. The bread that was lacking. Bread for the hungry. To wish for a mill meant to be hungry. With an endemic hunger, a permanent hunger.

"The mill is his childhood dream," the monk said. He smiled.

"Dreaming of a mill is not a serious thing," Nicholas said. "You should never dream about things you can't have. An Akathist, a Not Seated, until the end of the ages will never be able to own a mill."

The poet Ovid Panteleimon, who had been moved several years earlier by the other Akathist, the child monk, who chanted *Axion Estin* as he tended the monastery cows, was now moved by the Akathist who loved the earth and matter, as a man loves the body of his mistress.

When he talks with the Akathist monk, the poet is connected, like a receiver picking up signals from an antenna in heaven, to the soul of the Romanian people.

Listening now to the other Akathist brother, Ovid Panteleimon is connected to the earth. He feels and listens to the physical body of his country, exactly like a man feels the circulation of blood in the body of his beloved.

Ovid Panteleimon is the poet of Romania. This means he is the ear and mouth of his people. The most intimate part of his life is identified with the history of his people. When the Akathist brother dreams of a mill, the poet understands that the people are hungry, and that they want bread. The poet himself is truly hungry, even if his table is loaded with delicacies. The poet shouts with the rebels, weeps with the afflicted, endures captivity with prisoners, prays with monks, and loves those in love. A poet forms an integral part of his country, just as mountains, rivers, plains, and the climate and seasons are inseparable from the homeland. If a poet is killed, it is not a man that is killed, but a part of the living body of the nation is amputated. To kill a poet is to put out an eye, cut off an ear, or crush an arm of the nation. If the Thames were removed from England, London wouldn't be the same city. But if Shakespeare were taken away from England, then the British Isles would no longer be itself. That's worse than removing the Thames. Ovid Panteleimon is an integral part of Romania, just like the Danube and the Carpathians. The poet is more than the mountains and rivers of a country. He is the country itself. Ancient Greece, that is Homer, Euripides, Plato. The rest is secondary. And while the rest has disappeared, in spite of that Greece continues to live, for Aristotle, Sophocles, and Aeschylus are not dead. In order to know a country, a people, it is not its ministers and kings that must be known, but its prophets. The people of Israel, without possessing a single bit of land in their own right, have lived in history for thousands of years, in their prophets, in their Book. Romania is Ovid Panteleimon, the poet. And for his part, it's normal for him, the poet, to live his own life with the Akathist brothers. He prays with the monk, who is the heaven of Romania, and he dreams of a mill, to have bread, with Nicholas Akathist, who is the earth of Romania. Ovid Panteleimon loves them both, because he, the poet, can only exist through the two brothers. One is the heaven and the soul of the country, the other is the earth and the body of the country.

"Nicholas Akathist," Ovid Panteleimon says abruptly, "listen closely: you'll have your mill. It's me, the poet, who is telling you."

"I'll have it in my dreams, Professor," replies Nicholas.

"If you ardently long for it, and if you will it, you will be a miller," the poet says.

"Oh, Professor, you're talking like my brother the monk," Nicholas answers. "To wish for rain, to will it, doesn't mean having it."

"If you really want it, you'll have the mill of your dreams."

"If you give me an envelope with enough bills to buy it, then I'm certain of having it, Professor. But faith doesn't make wheat grow..."

Ovid Panteleimon, though quite proud, is not offended by the words of Nicholas. He finds it normal for a peasant to be a materialist. A peasant has no right to dream. He has to dig, to labor, to handle matter and to work with it.

"I swear to you, here by the walls of this monastery of the Dormition of the Virgin Mary, that you will have your mill, Nicholas, if you want it with your whole being. If you don't get it, it will be your fault. The fault of not having wanted it passionately enough."

"As far as my desire goes, have no fear, Professor. I've dreamed of having this mill since I came into the world, but desiring doesn't mean having . . . "

"Nicholas, have you read my books?" the poet asks brusquely. But he gets hold of himself and says, "Forgive me for asking you this question. It's stupid. You haven't read them. A peasant doesn't read poems. He writes them with his plow, on the earth in the spring. A peasant doesn't read poetry, he writes it himself with his scythe as he cuts the grass into green stanzas and places them in the meadow, like the verses of a sonnet. . . . Now I'll recount what I've written in one of my books. First tell me, Nicholas, have you ever heard the name of Columbus? He's the one who discovered the lands of America. This sailor named Columbus had decided to discover America. Exactly like you have decided to have a mill. So Columbus outfitted three ships and went to discover the lands he had dreamed of. He made all the sacrifices that a determined man can make to realize his dream. Sparing nothing. As he left, he entrusted himself to the Panagia Theotokos, to the all holy Mother of God, and he flew the flag of the Virgin next to the flag of his king. And he left. Ordeals beyond human strength awaited him. He withstood them. And he kept on sailing, straight ahead, dreaming of the lands of America and placing his trust in the Virgin.

"The Mother of God knew that the lands of America that Columbus wished to discover did not exist. But she could not leave so much courage, so much suffering, and so much faith go without recompense. So just to reward the courage and faith of Columbus, she created the two Americas. Solely to reward his tenacity and unshakable faith."

"The lands of America didn't exist before Columbus?" asks Nicholas, astonished.

"No, America did not exist before the departure of Columbus. There where North America, Central America, and South America are located today, there was only the water of the ocean. The Americas were created by the Mother of God, since the Mother of God always rewards those who really know how to believe and to will something. If you put your trust in the Panagia Theotokos, like Columbus, if you make as many sacrifices as he did, you will have your mill."

The cheeks of Nicholas Akathist were flushed with emotion and delight. He was determined to surpass the extraordinary sailor, Columbus, in faith, tenacity, and hope. He was determined to dazzle even the Mother of God with his faith and tenacity.

"You see, Nicholas, from the moment the Mother of God created that immense continent out of nothing to reward the courage of just one man, how easy it would be for her, the Mother of God, to give you a mill, here in the land of Vrancea. Compared to America, a little watermill is nothing at all for the Queen of Heaven. You will have your mill.... There is no doubt, absolutely no doubt.... I guarantee it."

The poet spoke in such a way that Nicholas Akathist hadn't the slightest doubt. It was now certain that he would be a miller. It was as though he already owned his mill, so sure was he of it. It belongs to poets to make every dream a reality.

Ovid Panteleimon took out of his pocket a little medallion with the image of Mary, the Mother of God, carrying Jesus in her arms. The Panagia holds the child with her left hand, and the fingers of her right hand are extended, pointing to Jesus. It is a copy of an icon painted by the evangelist Luke. This apostle was not only a man of faith filled with the Holy Spirit and a great writer, but was also a doctor and a painter. The icon of St. Luke is called *Hodegetria*, a Greek word meaning "she who shows the way," the Conductress, the Guide, La Condottiera.

"I'm giving this icon to you, Nicholas. It comes from Sicily. There, on that beautiful island, close to Palermo is a community of Albanians. In Sicily and Calabria there are more than a hundred thousand of them. They came to take refuge there when they fled from the Turks, five centuries ago. Before settling in Sicily, the Albanian refugees tried to disembark at all the ports of Italy. They were refused everywhere. They were asked, as they were turned away, who their leader was, their Condottiere. They never tired of answering that their Condottiera was Maria, the Mother of God. They were not lying. As exiles, they had no other head than the Mother of God. People who are everywhere turned away, who have no right of residence, who do not have permission to remain seated, the Akathists of every time and country, have no other leader than the Condottiera, the Mother of God. She alone is willing to take up the command of the Not Seated, the Akathists. Your leader, Nicholas, your true leader, is also the Condottiera. She alone. Look closely, the Mother of God is already showing you, in the medallion, the way that you're looking for. She is already your *Hodegetria*, your Condottiera. I consider this to be the most apt and the most beautiful title that men have given to the Mother of God, the Condottiera. This title describes how the *Hodegetria*, the Condottiera, came down to the beautiful land of Vrancea in the heart of Romania and took under her guidance the Akathist brothers and all the other Not Seated, all the other Always Standing, the poor and oppressed of the Carpathians..."

It's the poet Ovid Panteleimon who brought the Condottiera to the region of Vrancea.

From the day the Condottiera came to be with the Akathists of Vrancea, they became courageous. And that was a tremendous thing, because courage, dreams, and hope are like the sails of a ship. The bigger they are, the faster the ship goes. And above the sails of hope, on the mast of the ship of the Akathists of Vrancea, flies the standard of the Condottiera, their leader and commander.

Hope ran so deep in the hearts of the Akathists after enrolling under the command of the Condottiera that everything in the land went better. Chickens laid bigger eggs and more of them. Cows gave more milk. Of course, Nicholas Akathist still suffered from hunger, from poverty. Like the other Akathists. But now he was sure that proceeding along the route pointed out by the Condottiera, he would have a mill. And on that day there would be flour, bread, and polenta in the land of Vrancea. The living would be satisfied. And the dead too. They would have bread for funeral meals, for the hosts for the liturgy.

And the two Akathist brothers, the monk and the peasant, were no longer different from each other. After the Condottiera came down to be with them, they were of one mind in everything. The heaven of the monk Theophorus was mysteriously commingled with the earth of Nicholas. Heaven and earth were one thing. It was exactly like the Sunday liturgy, when heaven came down to earth, when the faithful mingled with the angels and saints, and couldn't distinguish between the things of the world and the things of heaven. Now heaven was descending into the land of Vrancea so that with the help of the Condottiera Nicholas could get a mill. So Nicholas Akathist's mill would belong to earth as well as to heaven. A mill for the living and the dead. For the world here below and for the world up above. It would grind grain for history and for eternity. Thanks to Nicholas Akathist's mill the world here below and the world on high would fuse and become only one paradise beginning here below, in time in the land of Vrancea, and ending in eternity, in heaven. No one doubted that, thanks to the Condottiera, they would one day have a mill belonging to both paradises...

◈◈◈◈◈

The next summer, Professor Ovid Panteleimon didn't come to the monastery of Vrancea for his vacation. War had broken out. This was in 1939. The Muscovites, that people from the eastern reaches of Europe and the steppes of Asia, who take their name from the city of Moscow, invaded the Romanian provinces of Bukovina and Bessarabia, which they annexed to their vast bicontinental empire.

Professor Ovid Panteleimon had been minister of culture. He had founded a journal. He put on the uniform of an officer. He was the one who mobilized hearts and set them on fire to fight against the Muscovite invaders. Liberty, he wrote, is the royal prerogative of men and angels. It is on account of liberty that men resemble their Creator, God. He who loses liberty, loses his status as a human creature; he becomes a slave capable of neither good nor evil. Twenty million Romanians, with no distinctions among classes, felt their hearts beat as one with the heart of the poet. It was a tragic moment in history. But it was at the same time a sublime moment in the life of a whole people who faced danger with a single body and a single soul. And this Romanian soul was one with heaven and earth.

Nicholas Akathist was called to military service. He wore the uniform of an infantryman. He was among the first to fight in the battlefield of the east. Peasants are always, in all wars, the first to be sent to the front lines, to the line of fire. Nicholas Akathist at this time realized that to win his mill, he also had to win the war against the invaders. So he fought harder than all the others. Because he fought for his mill.

Theophorus Akathist, in his monastery, redoubled his ascetic practices, his fasts and prayers, so that God would remain present to the Romanians in that time of misfortune. The monk Theophorus deprived himself of all food Wednesdays and Fridays, during which days he did not sleep at night and prayed ardently for victory against the Muscovites. For if they lost the war, the monks would lose the right to pray, to make heaven come down to earth. Romania was transformed into one sole blaze, in which one could no longer distinguish the poor from the rich, the Akathists from the Cathists, the lay people from monks, the young from the old, as they were all transfigured by combat and danger...

Nicholas Akathist was gravely wounded. He spent many weeks in the hospital. At the end of 1942, Corporal Nicholas Akathist was discharged due to his injury, decorated, and sent back to his village with a citation for his bravery and with a small, a very small, pension. He had the right, even though discharged, to wear his uniform with his medals and the badge awarded to those seriously wounded. He wore this with pride, every day, everywhere.

At the beginning of the month of August, 1943, Corporal Nicholas Akathist got a letter from his monk brother: "On the feast of the Dormition of Mary, the Mother of God, I will be ordained a priest. I beg you, my dear brother, to come to our holy monastery to participate in the celebration of the holy liturgy, during which I will receive the imposition of hands, the *cheirotonia*, and I will be raised to the dignity of the priesthood.

You will represent my family in the world, since besides you, dear brother Nicholas, I have no other relatives according to the flesh."

Nicholas Akathist polished his medals, ironed his uniform, made the brass buttons on his tunic and shoes gleam, and presented himself at the monastery. A stall was reserved for him in the church, next to the dignitaries, because he was a dignitary twice over, first as a hero who had given his blood for the defense of freedom, then as the only relative of the one who was to receive the Holy Spirit and be sanctified as a priest. Nicholas, that coarse peasant who loved matter, wept hot tears that burned his tanned face, when his brother, on his knees, was ordained to the priesthood. Nicholas then felt that he had definitively lost his brother. He was losing his brother in the world, here below, to gain a brother who would never die, in eternity. After the ceremony, Nicholas had lunch with the bishop, the hegumen, and the monks in the *Trapeza*, the monastery refectory. There was a long table of lime wood, very clean. They ate and drank from earthenware plates and jugs of water. During the meal, a monk stood and read the life of St. Mary of Egypt, that woman ascetic, who lived completely naked, all alone in the desert. At the end, they chanted the *Axion Estin*, gladdened in heart. Nicholas was very happy. Because the *Trapeza* is a refectory where all the walls are covered with icons, like the church, and they were fed with two kinds of bread, one for this life and one for eternity.

Nicholas said to the superior, "Very Reverend Father Hegumen, I am Theophorus's only relative. Our father was the *Christiac*, servant of the church. Now that Theophorus is a priest, we've advanced in the world. Give him permission to come and celebrate the divine liturgy in the village where we were born and to pray for our deceased, in the cemetery of the Akathists."

The hegumen agreed to the request of the corporal hero. So the two brothers, the soldier and the monk, left the enclosure of the Vrancea monastery around two in the afternoon on August 15, 1943. They left on foot. One beside the other. The monk like his brother was very moved. He was going as a priest to officiate in the church where he had been baptized, and where his father had been *Christiac*. It was in this church that Theophorus got his start in life. When, in order to have a right to participate in the funeral meal, he had to chant the funeral service for the deceased, beside his father. These dinners which were served after the burial were the only true meals of his childhood...

The two Akathist brothers were now happy. The people they met in the street, going through the villages of Vrancea, greeted them with respect and admiration as they went by. The two brothers were in uniform. The monk, Theophorus, wore a cassock, the uniform of heaven, and Nicholas wore the uniform of heroes of the earth, with his badge for bravery and his medals. They stopped at a spring. Nicholas gave his face a good washing. He adored springs, like all the riches of the earth. He was refreshed by the water in his mouth, on his face, hair, and chest, which he also washed after unbuttoning his tunic. He didn't do that just because of the heat. It was to savor the treasures of mother earth, because a spring is a treasure for travelers on foot, like them.

The day of the Dormition, August 15, it was hot and sultry, as it always was on that day. The dust of the road burned the soles of the feet of even those who wore shoes. The air was heavy, like honey heated up. The air was not only hot, but scented, perfumed, sweet due to the flowers in full bloom, with their pollen, and all their petals open to the sun.

"My mill will be called the Mill of the Condottiera,"

said Nicholas after deep draughts of water from the spring. "Do you like that name for my mill?"

Just then they heard a clap of thunder. The sky above the mountain had become black as tar. A few minutes later, a storm broke out over the land of Vrancea. The two brothers took shelter under a big oak, whose leaves protected them like a green metal roof.

"There are always storms on the feast of the Dormition," Nicholas said. And at that moment they heard the wheels of a cart led by a horse trotting along. Nicholas emerged from the shelter to stop the cart with a white horse and get a ride to the village. But even though he was in the middle of the road, in uniform, under a heavy downpour, the woman in the cart struck the horse with a whip. She passed Nicholas by, leaving him in the middle of the road, and disappeared as the horse galloped away.

"Bitch," Nicholas said. He didn't use swear words, because he had received communion at the monastery. But in spite of this communion, which he wanted to respect by staying calm and avoiding anger, his blood boiled. He went back to the shelter, under the oak, next to his brother.

"I'm soaked," said Nicholas. "She was alone in the cart. And she refused to stop. Even though she saw I was in uniform..."

The monk laughed. His brother's pride had been wounded.

Ever since he was discharged, Nicholas has thought himself a person of consequence. As he is the only young man seen walking around the village. All the girls look at him with a smile on their lips, since they see nothing but children and old people. Nicholas is highly regarded everywhere. Even policemen salute him, because he is decorated and was wounded in battle. He's a hero. The fact that a woman passed by, and refused to take him into her cart and would have crushed him if he hadn't gotten out of the way, hurt him. He adjusts his tunic. And he continues on his way, in a dark mood, on foot, beside his brother. The rain stopped as suddenly as it had begun. As they approach the Ozana River, which they're going to have to ford, Nicholas says to his brother, who stops and listens attentively, "The water is high...We won't be able to cross the river. Listen to the rumbling. If we can't get across, we'll turn back. We'll sleep at the monastery, and leave tomorrow before daybreak..."

"First we have to see whether we can cross," says Theophorus.

As he gets closer, he sees the swollen murky water which rushes by rumbling like thunder, carrying away tree trunks, big rocks like millstones. Rolling through the dirty waters, these rocks sound like canon fire when they knock against each other or hit the rocks along the river bank.... After each storm, no matter how short-lived, the waters of the Ozana, which is quite a small river, swell and overflow their bed, turning black, for the course of more than a kilometer. This is because all the water falling on the peaks of the Carpathians flows into the Ozana River. The waters rise in a fraction of a second. The Akathist brothers draw near. And when they see how difficult it would be to cross over, they're struck with fear. In the middle of the water, still rising, they find the cart and the white horse, driven by the woman who refused to give them a ride.

Without saying a word, Nicholas broke into a run, to go help the woman. In just a few seconds, the horse, the cart, and the unfortunate woman would be knocked over and carried off by the angry waters of the torrent.... As he ran, Nicholas threw his cap to his brother following behind. Without taking his eyes off the cart, he took off his jacket and threw that to him as well. He would have wished to remove his boots too, before throwing himself into the water. But he didn't have time to take them off. He went into the water shouting something to the woman, standing in her cart. Branches, tree trunks, and big stones were driven by the choppy black water. It had reached the horse's chest and continued to rise. The cart, three-quarters submerged, was on the verge of tipping over and being swept away. What held it back was the horse. But he was wobbling, as though he were drunk. The horse, his head lowered, was looking at the water coming nearer and nearer, as though hypnotized. He stretched out his neck as he bent over the water, fixing his eyes on it. And his whole body swayed. And when the horse swayed, the cart tottered. The beast and the cart would fall over at the same time and be carried off in a few seconds by the waves, just like the trees, shattered rocks, and branches . . .

Nicholas Akathist went into the water, which was up to his waist. He made headway with difficulty, stumbling several times. But he got to the cart. He shouted to the woman to stay calm and went toward the horse, careful not to lean on him. The horse was reeling from side to side, like the pendulum of a clock, one would have said. Nicholas was now up to his chest in water. When he got in front of the horse, he lifted up both his hands and covered the eyes of the animal with them, to blind him. The horse floundered, swaying even more. But Nicholas kept his hands in place. All this lasted but a few seconds, yet seemed like an eternity. Then the miracle happened. The animal wobbled less. His body and especially his legs became stable again. He got hold of himself and remained upright. When Nicholas felt that the horse's legs were steady, he pulled him to the further bank, still covering his eyes.

There was a simple explanation for this. As he forded the river, looking at the water which ran faster and faster beneath him, the horse became dizzy. He was afraid. And the more fearful he was of the water, the more he looked at it. And the more he looked at it, flowing at a frantic speed, the dizzier he got. When he was as though drunk with vertigo, the horse stopped. He bent his neck, his eyes wide open, gazing on the water rushing beneath him. And he awaited death. From drowning. By covering his eyes, Nicholas had kept him from seeing the water that stunned him. Nicholas Akathist knew everything about the weather, the earth, animals, all of nature.

When they got to the other side of the river, Nicholas Akathist gave the horse his sight back. The beast gave him a look of gratitude. The horse's eyes, hot like two cups of tea, gave off a vapor of fear, anguish, and gratefulness.

Then Nicholas went toward the woman. He wanted to scold her for having attempted to cross the rising river. He was angry with her for not stopping on the road, to take them in her cart, him and his brother. He wanted to tell her that what had happened to her, that adventure, that brush with death, was only a punishment for her lack of respect and charity toward a hero and a priest. But as soon as Nicholas saw the face of the woman, he no longer reproached her for anything. She wasn't a woman, but a child. In the cart was a girl of thirteen or fourteen. All wet. From the rain, from her tears, and from the waters of the torrent. She was crying. She had no thought for her rescuer. She turned around and started to look through the contents of the cart, filled with water. The more she searched through the cart, the more desperate she became. The water had damaged and dirtied the things she was transporting, now completely drenched.

"Oh, dear, that's a coffin you're carrying there, child?" asked Nicholas.

"It's my father's coffin," said the little girl. She was crying, more and more desperately, looking at the waterlogged coffin. Next to it were loaves of bread shaped like wheels. That was the bread for the funeral ceremony. The loaves were big like the wheels of the cart. There were candles. They floated in the water. The bread looked pasty. And the black shoes of the dead man were also floating in the water that filled the cart like a bathtub. There were pieces of crepe. Everything was soiled, soaked through, ravaged.

"Tomorrow is the burial of my father," the girl wailed. She wrung out her skirt like a rag. For she was in her cart, filled with water, exactly like being in a bathtub with water up to her knees.

"Why were you sent to get the coffin, all by yourself? That's not a job for a young girl," Nicholas scolded her. His fine shoes and his uniform trousers with red braid were wet. He was furious at the girl. It was because of her that all this had happened!

"I am alone," the girl explained. "There was no one else to make the trip to the city..."

Nicholas then understood the tragedy. "Now you're an orphan?" he asked.

"Yes, sir."

"And it's your father who died? The coffin is for him?"

"Yes, sir."

The girl explained that she had lived alone with her father. She had neither mother, nor brothers or sisters. No family. Only her and her father. And he had just died. And the next day the burial was supposed to take place. And now she didn't know how that could be done, since the beautiful black casket was full of water, the wheel-shaped breads were like mush, and all the articles for the ceremony were ruined. She wept. Suddenly, she looked at Nicholas in the eye and said to him, "I am Sabina, Mr. Akathist.... You are well acquainted with me. Why are you asking me what happened? Since you're well aware that my father died yesterday. You were friends with him."

Nicholas looked at the girl. Closely. He didn't recognize her.

"You're Sabina, the daughter of the miller Stoica?"

He certainly knew that the old miller had a child, quite a young one. And now this child had grown. Very quickly, like the waters of the torrent. She was an adolescent now, almost a woman. He didn't recognize her. As the little crystalline Ozana River is no longer recognized when its waters rise after rainfall.

At that moment, Nicholas Akathist realized that he was the object of a prodigious event. He ran as close to the water as he could and shouted to his brother on the opposite bank, quite loudly, so that he would hear, as the waters made a terrible noise.

"Theophorus, keep my cap and jacket, and dry them out tonight. Spend the night at the monastery. You'll come to the village tomorrow, after the waters subside.... Bring me the tunic tomorrow. You'll find me at the mill. Do you understood what I'm telling you? I won't be at our house. Go directly to the mill.... You'll find me there."

Waving goodbye to his brother, Nicholas got into the cart. He emptied the water out of the coffin. He set the bread to dry out. He gathered the candles and all the other things. Then he pushed the girl over to the left. He took up the reins. As though the cart had been his. And he set out for the mill. He was really amazed. Exactly like saints who are the subjects of miracles. Like Saint Paul, who was thrown to the ground. Nicholas knew just one thing with certitude, that the Panagia Condottiera, who had spoken to him the first time at the Vrancea monastery, through the mouth of the poet Ovid Panteleimon, promising him a mill, had kept her word. Because now the Condottiera has really sent him the mill. The Condottiera has just given the mill to Nicholas Akathist, in the middle of the water, in the midst of the torrent. The Condottiera had put Nicholas yet again to the test. She wanted to see if he was going to plunge into the water. If he was willing to face death. Like Columbus. If he was courageous. If he knew how to manage the horse beset with dizziness and if he could save the girl. It was only after she had imposed this last trial that the Condottiera, the Mother of God, gave the mill of the Stoicas to Nicholas. For now the mill was his. It was a gift from heaven. A gift accompanied by a coffin. He would provide a very fine burial for the miller. That was certain. And the mill he was getting was accompanied by the girl. His future wife.

Nicholas turned toward Sabina and looked at her closely.

"How old are you now, Sabina?"

"Fourteen, sir," she replied without looking at him. But she was no longer crying, because she too was no longer alone. She had received in the middle of the water a husband and a miller.

"Only fourteen?" asked Nicholas. He thought fast, to get married a girl had to be at least fifteen. The Mother of God was incapable of sending him a girl who was not of marriageable age. The Condottiera does everything very well. She never makes a mistake.

"I'll be fifteen in six months!" Sabina clarifies.

Nicholas's face lights up. The Condottiera has imposed the period of mourning on the girl. For a girl must be in mourning for her father at least six months. During this six-month delay, required by civil law and by the law of custom imposing a time of mourning, Nicholas would put the mill in order. He was very familiar with it. Old Stoica had been ill for quite some time. The mill wasn't working any more. The river would have to be dredged, the dams of the lake repaired, and, most of all, the four large millstones, out of service, would have to be replaced. That was a huge undertaking. At least six months would be needed for all that. Since on the day of the wedding, the mill wheel would have to revolve. The mill would have to function. Of course, there would be musicians, but the principal music would be the mill wheel turning round...

Timidly, out of the corner of his eye, Nicholas looks at the girl at his side who will become his wife. He doesn't need to ask the girl for her consent. No, that would be a sacrilege. She was given to him by the Condottiera Panagia, the Mother of God, in the middle of the water, after a final test. Nicholas sees that the girl is very beautiful. Her cheeks are rosy, like cherry blossoms, especially after crying. But in ascertaining the beauty of his wife-to-be, he realizes that he has committed a sacrilege. Sabina was given to him along with the mill by the Mother of God, to reward his courage and determination, and his injuries in the battle against the Muscovites. Exactly as America was created and given to Columbus as a reward for his courage. Nicholas has no right to appraise the value and beauty of the present. Every gift should be received with gratitude, without being examined.

The cart with the white horse, driven by Nicholas Akathist, arrives at the mill. The candles beside the head of the dead miller are lighted. Then Nicholas unloads the coffin. And he begins the burial preparations. He asks nothing of Sabina. He is at home. Neither does the girl ask for anything. She finds that things are restored to order with Nicholas there. He got a bed ready in the loft of the mill. He slept. In his mill. The next day the monk Theophorus Akathist arrived. With the cap and tunic of his brother. For the burial ceremony, Nicholas wore all his decorations and walked beside

Sabina, behind the coffin. It was Nicholas Akathist who led the funeral procession. Everyone found this normal. No one asked any questions. For everyone, Nicholas Akathist was the new miller. And Sabina, the orphaned daughter, would be the miller's wife. It was only a matter of a few details to take care of. Waiting six months until the time of mourning was over and the girl reached the age of fifteen, as the marriage laws required . . .

◌◌◌◌◌

The very evening of the burial, Nicholas Akathist wrote a long letter to his friend, the minister, professor, and poet Ovid Panteleimon: "Your Excellency, now I have seen with my own eyes that what is written in holy books is true and that God speaks to men through the mouths of poets and prophets. The Condottiera, the Mother of God, promised me, from your lips, a mill, as she promised Columbus the land of the Americas. Yesterday, for the feast of the Dormition, I received the mill you had foretold. This is how it happened: The Mother of God led me to the bank of the Ozana River. There the Condottiera unleashed a storm. A storm out of the ordinary. In a few moments the torrential waters rose, swollen and unrelenting. The Mother of God said to me, 'In the middle of the water there is a cart with a white horse, a coffin, and a young girl. The horse is dizzy and is going to fall over in a few seconds, and the water will carry them all off. You have a few seconds to show your courage and save them. If you save them, when you get to the other side of the river, I will give you as a reward the mill that I promised you through the lips of my poet Panteleimon. What is more, I will give you the girl in the cart as your wife.' That is what the Mother of God told me. I wasn't dreaming. My brother, who had been ordained a priest that very day, was with me. Because the Mother of God wanted this miracle to be witnessed by a holy man. That is why my brother was there. To testify to what he had seen. I jumped into the water. As the Condottiera had asked me, I saved the cart, horse, coffin, and girl. And the Mother of God told me, when she had witnessed my bravery, 'Nicholas, you are my favorite soldier. I am giving you the mill. The coffin of the old miller is in the cart. Do him the honor of burying him with dignity. Then you will repair the mill with the help of my poet Panteleimon, whom I made a minister. And six months later, you will marry Sabina, the girl whom I put in the cart.' And what I had been commanded came to pass. Now, still following the orders of the Condottiera, I ask for your help in putting the mill in working order. It would be a great sin not to execute the Condottiera's orders to the letter. I have made a complete list for you of all the items necessary to get the mill functioning, the mill that will be called the Mill of the Condottiera from now on. Most important are the four millstones, the exact dimensions of which I have noted. On account of the war, these millstones cannot be obtained in Romania. I beg you to order them yourself from Germany, from the town of Leipzig, at the address I have indicated. You are not only the poet of the Condottiera, but also a minister, so you will be able to have the millstones sent to me in time. For on my wedding day, the mill has to be in operation for the happiness of men on earth and for the glory of heaven .... I have already ordered, through my father and brother Theophorus, an icon, a mosaic, depicting the Condottiera. A second icon, painted on wood, will be taken to the village church. We will have them blessed on the day of the wedding, in your presence. I am certain that you will come to the wedding as best man. The Condottiera in heaven will be very happy to have you as our witness. Since it is from your lips, the lips of a poet, that she promised the mill and foretold the miracle that has just taken place . . . "

After sending the letter, Nicholas started on the repairs. He wanted to complete the dredging of the river before winter. He rebuilt the dam. He worked day and night. He didn't even look at Sabina. Since she would not be his wife for six months. And only then would he look at her.

When snow covered the mountains and plains and the land of Vrancea was all white, as though robed in a bridal gown, the millstones arrived from Germany by train. The day of the Theophany, January 6, the icon of the Panagia Condottiera was placed on the front wall of the mill. It was a beautiful icon, an enameled mosaic, the work of the icon writers of the Vrancea monastery, after the prototype of the *Hodegetria*, painted by St. Luke. The wall was beautiful like the facade of a church. The icon was created in accordance with very specific canons and rules on the *hermeneia*, where it is stated: "The image of the Mother of God must be different from all the images of the visible world. The depiction of her image should help to elevate our minds to celestial realities, and, thanks to the image of the All-Holy Woman, enable us to glimpse eternal beauty here below. The painter should thus turn his eyes away from earthly things and lift up his eyes as he paints, and, of all that is beautiful, limit himself to celestial beauty."

The icon of the *Hodegetria* Condottiera on the wall of the mill is of the dimensions specified by the canons: "She is of average stature and age. Her hair is the color of wheat and her face has a golden cast. Her eyes are very beautiful, her eyebrows and eyelashes are long, her nose of average size, her hands are delicate, with long fingers. She is dressed with a pious modesty, clothed only with a *maphorion,* which emphasizes her face, luminous like the sun and the inestimable treasures she has been showered with."

All the preparations were made. In the spring, when the waters of the Ozana River were freed from their prison of ice, where they had been held captive all winter, they encountered the splendid wheel of the mill, a giant wheel which they began to turn, throwing off on all sides sprays of white foam, like scarves, immaculate as the veils of brides.

Then, also for the Akathist wedding, the cherry trees, apple trees, and all the vegetation of nature was clothed with flowers, dressed in white. Even the stones of the crags were overlaid with green, white, and red, all the floral colors. Then the poet Ovid Panteleimon arrived. As befit a poet of the Condottiera, surrounded by all the dignitaries of the region of Vrancea. The bishop himself officiated at the wedding, encircled by seven priests and by deacons. It wasn't every day that a man who had received his bride as a gift from the Mother of God was married. And it wasn't every day that a minister and poet went down to a village to serve as best man for a peasant miller. For three days and three nights the marriage of Nicholas Akathist, the miller, to Sabina Stoica was celebrated. She was dazzling, as she was not an ordinary bride. The poet Panteleimon explained to Sabina that she was not only a beautiful girl and a beautiful miller's wife, but that first and foremost she was the gift that heaven gave to Nicholas Akathist in order to compensate all the Akathists, all the Not Seated, all the proletariat for their endurance, their hunger, their humiliations .... In giving the mill to an Akathist, the Mother of God symbolically nourished all those who had been hungry for centuries and centuries, showing them too that she hadn't forgotten them and had protected them from heaven above. And just as Nicholas Akathist had received a mill, from which flour flowed as from a spring, the other Akathists would also be compensated if they were valiant and faithful to the Condottiera like Nicholas was. And all the Akathists would one day have, as the reward for their suffering, mills and beautiful wives....

Meanwhile, they admired the splendid mill of the Condottiera. Everything about it was beautiful. As in a church, because the mill was the result of collaboration between men and divinity. And because men and heaven had worked hand in hand for its realization, the mill belonged as much to heaven as to earth. It was a kind of vestibule leading from history to eternity, a mill belonging to both paradises, the one above and the one below...

The opening of the mill and the wedding took place in the spring of 1944. A few months later, August 23, 1944, at dawn, before sunrise, troops of invading Muscovites entered the land of Vrancea. All Romania was occupied by foreign soldiers. In their wake, the grass no longer grew. Wherever they went, there was only scorched earth, tears, and mourning. Even the birds, out of pity for the Romanians, stopped singing.

As soon as they came to the village of the Akathists, the Muscovites arrested the miller and sent him to prison. They proceeded in the same fashion in all the villages. Sabina was arrested and raped by the Muscovites and their collaborators innumerable times. Then she too was sent to prison. The monks of the Vrancea monastery were all arrested, and sent to labor camps. Theophorus Akathist was imprisoned with the other monks.

All the land was confiscated. All the houses. The conquered people no longer had anything. The masters of the people were the collaborators of the occupiers, the

PC. They, the wardens, were the ones who were given the power of life and death over the herd of conquered people. Romania was called the PRR, which really means the Penitentiary Republic of Romania. The borders were fenced in with barbed wire. The regime of the citizens was like that of any penitentiary. It was the wardens, collaborators of the occupier, who determined whether people would live or die, where and in what capacity they would work, and what they would eat and when. The people were reduced to the condition of a herd of animals. While the guards of this penitentiary country had every right and power, the men and women who lived in the Penitentiary Republic of Romania had exactly the same rights that sheep and cows had in a herd. The citizens owed absolute submission to the Party of the Collaborators, which herded them like cows, made them work like oxen and horses, fleeced them, and took away the fruit of their labor and their little ones. When they had had enough of them, they killed them, as animals are killed for their hide, their flesh, or to get rid of them.

When they entered the land of Vrancea, the Muscovite invaders were guided by Mavid Zeng, the merchant of hides and dead animals, the flayer of carcasses, and by other collaborators of the occupier. These collaborators of the enemy were the ones who caused most of the tears and blood to flow in the region. They were worse than the Muscovites. And they had absolute power. The occupiers let them do as they liked. That was the old method of the Muscovites. This strange people, when they were nomads, made a discovery, thanks to which they survived in history. The Muscovite nomads discovered how to train animals as their auxiliaries. As soon as they trained dogs, they no longer had to be busied with taking care of their flocks. When they transitioned to a settled existence, the Muscovites applied to their human communities the same laws they had used for animals in the times of their nomad life. So the Muscovite people were scourged with the knout (a terrible whip, of their invention) like herds of animals. The Muscovite society was divided into two classes, the herd of people and their keepers. To keep watch over men who were like animals of labor, they no longer utilized dogs like they did when it was a matter of horses, cows, and sheep. For herds of men, the Muscovites always employed a people of a different race, the Cossacks. They made up the great Muscovite guard. They were the police force and the secret police. When they invaded Romania, the Muscovites formed a pack of ferocious guards, recruited from among criminals, convicts, adventurers, and the riffraff of society. Incorporated into the PC, the Party of the Collaborators, they were the absolute masters of the poor vanquished Romanian people. They were all of the same class as Mavid Zeng and Zid Caracal. One could hope for no justice, no compassion on the part of the collaborators. As the Chinese killed the birds in the sky so they could have more grain, so the collaborators of the occupying forces of Penitentiary Romania killed so they could pillage. Almost half the people of Vrancea perished or disappeared in the initial months of the Muscovite occupation, under orders from Mavid Zeng.

In their infernal labor camps, the Akathist brothers, like all the survivors in Vrancea, wore on their chest the icon of the Condottiera, the Theotokos, the Panagia, the Mother of God, who was more than ever their only hope and their only leader.

And the Condottiera, just as she had given the mill to Nicholas Akathist, worked a miracle for all the faithful who lived in the Penitentiary Republic of Romania.

This miracle occurred on March 5, 1953 at 9:50.

✐✐✐✐✐

The morning of March 5, the Grand Muscovite, the man who could boast of having killed the most men since the world had existed, for he had killed with a submachine gun, day and night, for forty years, collapsed at the feet of his lieutenants, poisoned by his own venom. He writhed in pain, thrashing about on the carpet like epileptics in their atrocious suffering, for more than an hour. Not one of his lieutenants troubled himself over the tyrant tormented by pain like a poisoned dog. The Grand Muscovite died, without anyone lifting a finger for him. His lieutenants immediately began to fight over who would succeed as the head of the great bicontinental empire of the Muscovites. It was a bloody and bitter struggle that lasted two years. The winner was a Ukrainian, a large man. The first thing the new fat Grand Muscovite did was to visit the marvelous countries of the West. Then the Muscovites at home were told things unheard of about America and Europe. During the Grand Muscovite's reign of terror, no one had been authorized to travel abroad. Now that his lieutenants had taken over, they continually traveled from one country to another. In the United States of America, the Yankees, the craftiest merchants in the world, knowing the new Grand Muscovite was a peasant from Ukraine, had him visit the farms of the United States.

The Americans showed the Grand Muscovite cows, beautiful, big, and buxom like the singers of the Opera of Moscow, and which gave thousands of liters of milk a year. The udders of these American cows were like artesian fountains from which milk flowed almost without stop, as in the paradise of Muslims. The Grand Muscovite, filled with wonder, admired the corn with kernels bright as gold and big as hazelnuts. He saw heads of wheat bigger than sparrows. The soil of the United

States of America produced a hundred times more wheat, corn, and beans than the soil of the Muscovites. The Grand Muscovite, who loved fields and livestock and who had a passion for agriculture, wept when he beheld such fertility. He invited American farmers to his country as advisors. They then explained to the Grand Muscovite that the principal requirement for wheat to grow better, for cows to give more milk, and for the soil to produce a hundred times more was for the people in charge of all this to be free. Forced labor and the subjection of men reduce production. Back in Moscow, the Grand Muscovite ordered that the people be freed. In their land, it works like this: they order you to be free at gunpoint. When the Muscovites became Christian, they did it under orders, under the threat of bayonets. The police led the people like a herd to the bank of the great river. They ordered the people to disrobe, to go into the water, and at the command of the priest prisoners abducted from the Greeks, to immerse their heads in water three times. This was the collective baptism of the Muscovites. Those who refused or got there late, or who did not put their heads under water at the signal of the priest, were beaten to death by the Cossacks. It was now not a matter of becoming Christian, since the Muscovites had departed from Christianity. Always by order of the Grand Muscovite and with the aid of Cossacks. Now the people got the order to become free. With kicks in the rear, they released all the prisoners from the camps and prisons. They had to follow orders and become free from one day to the next, under pain of death. In freeing the captives, the Grand Muscovite hoped that milk would flow from the udders of the cows as from a spring. He waited for the soil to produce three harvests a year. Because under the threat of revolvers and the knout, all the Muscovites were now free.

A few years later, due to famine, they also ordered the peoples occupied by the Muscovites to become free, within the confines of their Penitentiary Republic. Romania received orders to free the people, under the surveillance of the collaborators, from the enclosure of their penitentiary camps. Thus Sabina Akathist got the order in 1956 to leave her labor camp and to conduct herself as a free woman, after twelve years of imprisonment. At the same time the monk Theophorus Akathist was also liberated. And because he didn't know where to go, since the monastery had been closed, he returned to the village. Nicholas Akathist, who spent twelve years in jail for the crime of being a miller, after several months was liberated in 1958. He received orders to work at the mill on behalf of the Party of the Collaborators, to whom the confiscated mill belonged.

Each year, on August 23, they lead the Romanian people like a big herd into the streets and obligate them to shout that they are happy and that they love the collaborators and the foreign occupier.

At around the same time the Chinese opened their sky to the birds which they had banned from their territory and from the sky of their republic. For they had expelled and killed all the sparrows because they ate too much grain. The birds were useless beaks. But when there were no more birds in China to eat the worms and insects, these creatures devoured the harvests. The soil of China no longer yielded anything. All the crops were compromised. In spite of their thoroughness, the Chinese hadn't succeeded in exterminating all the insects and worms. So they recalled the birds. They realized that the useless beaks were indispensable. In like fashion, the Muscovites and the collaborators of the countries conquered by them found out that the people they had locked up, killed, and imprisoned were useful. Indispensable. And at the same time the Chinese who in order not to die of hunger recalled the birds to China, the Party of the Collaborators along with the occupier of Romania, summoned the people from prisons, from camps, from exile, to work with them. Because these undesirables were indispensable. Exactly like the birds of China.

The life of the Akathist brothers was better now. The regime was still herd-like. Men were still treated like herds of beasts by the collaborators. Romania was still a Penitentiary Republic. But the prisoners had a bit more liberty. This second phase in the life of occupied Romania did not last long. In 1964 twenty years after the Muscovite occupation, the collaborators were all multimillionaires. They were plump like pigs. They lived in all the towns forbidden to the people. They had their stores, their food, their water mains. The Party of the Collaborators lived like a different people in the midst of the Romanian people. There were collaborators who owned up to ten Rolls-Royces for their personal use. The wives of the collaborators took planes like people take taxis, every other day to go to the hairdresser in Vienna, Rome, or Paris. The collaborators kept to themselves. Completely cut off from the rest of the country. They mated only among themselves. It was another race, another caste, another universe. The people, always led like a herd, possessed nothing. Absolutely nothing. Except a right to the whip.

The day that everything in the Romanian land belonged to them, the collaborators reintroduced the right to private property. Because they wanted everything they had confiscated from the people to belong to them legally, personally, so that they could leave to their children the castles, the lands, and the wealth they had stolen. So they reinstituted private property. Everything was put under their personal names. The whole country. Even if there were a change of regime, going from the herd-like, collectivist system to the capitalist system, they would always be the masters, because they possessed full ownership, in their names, of the country, as private property.

Requisitions were changed into benevolent gifts. So it was that at the beginning of the month of August, 1964 the miller Nicholas Akathist received a visit from Zid Caracal, who was in charge of the village.

"You should give over your mill to the party," proposed Zid Caracal.

Nicolas Akathist was astonished at such an invitation. He replied, "But you took my mill away from me, and you've had it for twenty years.... I no longer own a mill. I work there as a laborer. I'm your worker. How can I give you what I don't own anymore? I no longer have a mill."

"Do you trust the collaborators?" asks Zid Caracal.

"I'm compelled to, really," Nicholas Akathist answers.

"The Party of Collaborators has decided to reinstitute private property."

"You're giving me back my mill?"

"We are giving you back your mill," Zid Caracal answers. "That's why I'm here."

Nicholas Akathist falls to his knees, facing east, and says, "Panagia Condottiera, thank you for returning the mill to me. Our mill, yours and mine ... "

"We give you back your mill, but you make a commitment to make a gift of it to the Party.... Do you understand?"

"No," answers Nicholas. "I don't understand at all, Your Comradeship. You have taken my mill and you have it. Why return it to me, to take it away from me again? Keep it, that's simpler."

"No," Zid Caracal says. "We don't want to hear it said that we've despoiled the people. That we've taken the property of the people by force. No, that can't be said any more. We restore all that we've taken. To everyone."

"The owners, you've killed them," cries Sabina, as she returns to the mill. "You can't restore anything to the dead."

"To the dead, no. We can no longer do it. But we're restoring their property to the living, to the heirs of those who have died in the course of the past twenty years, since we came to power . . . "

Zid Caracal puts the deed to the mill, owned by Stoyan Stoica, Sabina's late father, on the table. And the marriage certificate of Sabina and Nicholas Akathist, by which marriage he inherited the mill.

"Here is the deed to your mill," Zid Caracal says. "I keep my promises."

"So we're once again the owners of our mill?" Sabina asks.

"Yes, you are, once again. But you promise me to make a gift of it to the Party. As a testimony of admiration for the collaborators. Saying that you are convinced that you find it more just for the mill to belong to the Party than to an individual."

"You can kill us," Sabina cries. "We will never do such a thing. Never. You have martyred us for twenty years and you want us to give you our mill as a testimony of gratitude! As we thank you for the torture!"

"You no longer own the mill," Zid Caracal says. "You make us a present of something that, in any case, no longer belongs to you."

"Out of the question," Sabina answers. "Rather death!"

"Listen, Sabina, his Comradeship Zid Caracal is right. We give the party a thing that no longer belongs to us . . . . We lose nothing. We can sign this paper. What do we lose? . . . "

"Sooner death," cries Sabina. "They took my mill by force, and they're keeping it by force, by violence . . . . They'll never get the donation of the mill. Never. Sooner death. Sooner set it on fire."

"Don't be stubborn, Sabina," Nicholas says. "In actual fact, what His Comradeship is asking us to do has no importance for us."

"It has the greatest importance," Sabina says. "It's the same as what they did to me. When the village was invaded, the Muscovites and collaborators raped me, in front of my mill. Once, twice, countless times. But I, before God, before my husband, before my own self, and before the whole world, consider myself pure. As though I were a virgin. Since they took me by force, against my will, that cannot be imputed to me as a sin. And if now they ask me to confirm in writing that I was possessed dozens of times by the Muscovites and collaborators through my will and desire, then I'm the biggest prostitute in the world.... The filthiest and most despicable of women.... As a human being, you see the difference. As long as the will of a man is not engaged, he is pure. What they did to my body and my mill doesn't count. It was against my will. But if you sign our mill over to them, it's as though I had signed that I wanted to be possessed by the soldiers who invaded my country and who violated me..."

And taking the bread knife from the table, with the words *Unsere tägliche Brot* on the handle, which had been given them by the manufacturers of the millstones, Sabina, threatening Nicholas, her husband, said to him, "Nicholas, if you give the mill to these people who have reduced us to an animal state, and who are criminals, I'll kill you with this knife by my own hand."

Then she slammed the door as she left.

Zid Caracal also left. This happened on Thursday, August 6, the feast of the Transfiguration.

∽✐✐✐✐✐✐∽

August 23, two weeks after this scene, Nicholas gave his mill to the collaborators of the Muscovites, in the public square, before the people assembled for the National Holiday. As Zid Caracal had asked. Two hours later, Nicholas Akathist was stabbed in the back. In front of his mill. Exactly as his wife had promised him. With the same knife she had threatened him with. At the crime scene, the brother of the victim, the monk Theophorus, was arrested. It was all clear now. The monk was the one who killed his brother, with the knife Sabina gave him, at the instigation of the young woman. On account of the mill.

VI

The Monk and the Woman
Face to Face

THE MILITIA CAME TO THE MILL during the night and removed the body of the miller Nicholas Akathist. In the dust of the road there remained the blood of the victim and the stubs of the candles which had burned for him all evening. Sabina Akathist, the wife of the murdered miller, was arrested at nightfall and confined in the Castel Vaca.

As soon as the people heard the news of the murder, there was terrible sorrow in the land of Vrancea. Not because of the death of the miller. For twenty years, since the country had been occupied, people had been massacred just like flies are killed. Death no longer made any impression. Nothing made an impression.

But the fact that a monk, a holy man, a priest, could have killed his own brother to take his wife, that was something that could not be endured. Holiness was the only thing that the Muscovite invaders had not succeeded in confiscating and banning. And here sanctity itself was sullied. The people no longer had anything. It was like a poor girl whose only treasure was her virginity. If she loses it, she has nothing. Now the virginity of the Church was lost. A monk had become a murderer and fratricide. The land of Vrancea had already lost the earth; if it now lost heaven, what would the land and its inhabitants do? Even if the people didn't go to church as often as they should have, even if they didn't say the Our Father before going to bed, they had heaven as their source of hope. And now heaven had fallen on

them. It had crashed like a dome of glass. Because they
had desecrated it. Heaven itself was desecrated. While
the inhabitants of Vrancea staggered from what had
just happened, the monk Akathist and his accomplice
were brought face to face in the office of His Exalted
Comradeship Mavid Zeng.

That night the priest monk as well as the woman
have aged several years. They are pale, they have dark
circles under their eyes, as they have not slept. Sabina is
a woman of short stature. At thirty-five, she is already
an old woman, with gray hair. The twelve years she
has spent in prison have left deep lines, like wounds,
on her face. She has cried all night, in her cell, in the
basement of Castel Vaca. She has wept for the death
of her miller. She never called Nicholas "my husband,"
but "my miller." And he always called her his "miller's
wife." Even after losing their mill. Her eyes are red
from crying. After wailing all night, her voice is hoarse.
Now it's not a matter of her immense sorrow, of her
widow's grief, but of her crime.

Mavid Zeng opens the dossier. He says, "We have
collected a huge amount of evidence that unequivocally
confirms that you, Sabina Akathist, had threatened to
kill your husband for several weeks, almost daily. You
gave voice to threats even in public. You shamelessly
took hold of a long knife as you said that if your husband made a gift of the mill to the Party, you would
kill him with your own hand, sticking that knife into
his back. That is what was done. Sabina Akathist, do
you recognize this knife?"

Mavid Zeng shows it to her. Its blade is more than
twenty centimeters long. The blade is stained with
blood. On the handle is written *"Unsere tägliche Brot,"*
"Our daily bread." When she sees the knife, tears once
more run down Sabina's face.

"That is our knife," she says. "It's the bread knife ... "

"This is the knife you threatened your husband with, isn't it?"

"Yes, Your Exalted Comradeship!" Sabina confirms.

"You threatened to stab him in the back with it if he gave the mill to the Party, didn't you?"

"Yes, Your Exalted Comradeship, I threatened him."

"On August 23 your husband officially gave the mill to the Party. He made the donation before the people. From the official platform. Two hours later, you killed him, as you had threatened to do, didn't you?"

"No, Your Exalted Comradeship, I did not kill my miller."

"You didn't kill him with your own hand, as you had boasted of doing. This is true. The experts are categorical: 'It was a man who plunged the knife into the back of the victim.' But it was at your instigation. How did it happen?"

"I do not know, Your Comradeship." Sabina weeps.

"I'm going to tell you myself how it happened. You gave the knife to your brother-in-law, asking him to stick it into the back of your husband. Is that true or not?"

"No, Your Comradeship. I did not kill my husband. And I did not ask anyone to kill him. I loved my husband!"

"Do you acknowledge that you said in public that you would kill him if he handed over the mill?"

"I threatened him. But those were words. Just words. No more."

"Tell us how and when you threatened him."

"I no longer remember," says Sabina. "You know that better than I do. The first time was August 6, feast of the Transfiguration. Zid Caracal came to ask my miller and me to make a gift of our mill to the Party. It was then that I got angry, and took the knife from the table, and threatened to kill him if he did that."

"A deed that was carried out exactly as you have said. Right after the donation, he was stabbed with that same knife. Was the monk, your brother-in-law, present when you threatened your husband with death?"

"No," Sabina replies.

"He lived with you at the mill?"

"Not exactly," Sabina answers. "He was at the church day and night."

"Did the monk or didn't he live at the mill with you?"

"Yes," Sabina answers. "He returned from the labor camps at the same time I did. And when he left, after twelve years of detention, he found the monastery closed. So he came to the mill. And he lived there. But he spent his days and nights at the church."

"You were all alone at the mill during this time?" You and he lived together, just you two, at the mill? Since your husband was freed two years later, wasn't he?"

"Nicholas was freed two years later," says Sabina.

"During those two years, you and your brother-in-law had a liaison?"

"No!" cries Sabina.

"Yes! You were the mistress of your brother-in-law! . . . "

"Father Theophorus is a holy man. How can you say that I was the mistress of a saint? Do saints have mistresses?"

"We've seen what the holiness of monks is like, with Rasputin. We're been enlightened about these things . . . . What did you do the day of the murder? Why didn't you take part in the National Holiday?"

"Caracal will tell you why. I had given notice to him that I would not go to the August 23 parade. Even if they shot me."

"When did you tell Comrade Zid Caracal that you wouldn't take part in the holiday?"

"August 22, in the evening. His Comradeship Zid Caracal came to the mill. It was already getting dark. He brought my husband, as a gift from the Party, a complete national costume. Pants, shirt, jacket, shoes, belt . . . everything. He told my husband that he had to get dressed in the new clothes. To look good when he was on the official platform next to Your Exalted Comradeship, to read the act of donation of the mill."

"And you told Comrade Caracal that you would abstain from participating in the celebration?"

"I said that even if I were shot, I would not go to see and hear my husband give our mill to the Party."

"So you stayed hidden all day and when your husband got back to the mill, you killed him, with the complicity of your lover and brother-in-law, the monk. Exactly as you had threatened to do."

"I did not kill my miller."

"You have no alibi, no way to defend yourself. How was it that the knife that was at the mill in the morning, on the table, was found in the back of the victim? No one could have entered the mill to take it. Except you and your brother-in-law. The mill was locked."

Sabina is silent. The knife really was on the table the morning of the crime. Where it always was. And to enter the mill, no one had the key except her, Nicholas, and Father Theophorus.

"The knife was on the table in the morning," Sabina says. "It is true. But I don't know who took it. It wasn't me."

"Come a little closer," orders Mavid Zeng. He makes a sign to Father Theophorus to draw nearer.

"You left the celebration at five o'clock in the afternoon, didn't you?"

"Yes, Your Exalted Comradeship. I left the celebration at five o'clock in the afternoon."

"This was to go back to the village and kill your brother, wasn't it?"

"No, Your Comradeship. I left early, since I marched with the consumptives. Priests had all been moved to their column for the parade. The parade of the consumptives ended at five o'clock. The sick had to get back to their hospital beds by six o'clock.... We priests were ordered to go back home as well. Like the consumptives."

"Were you present at your brother's official donation of the mill?"

"Yes, Your Exalted Comradeship. I saw my brother get up on the platform. To your right. And I heard him read the letter presenting his mill to the glorious Party of the Collaborators, who assisted the Muscovites in inaugurating a new society in our country."

"Were you happy that your brother was giving his mill to the Party?"

"Neither happy nor unhappy, Your Exalted Comradeship. I myself am a monk. It's not up to me to judge the things of the world."

"Did your brother do a good thing in giving the mill to the Party? Answer yes or no."

"Our holy fathers say that he who loves the world automatically loves the possibility of ruin. If a monk happens to lose some material thing, he should welcome this loss with joy and gratitude, considering that he has gotten rid of a worry. This is my opinion about the loss of the mill and any material thing whatever. That's the teaching from the *Apophtegms* of the fathers, which I keep to. But this opinion is that of a monk. Good for monks."

"You were present for the donation of the mill then. You saw your brother go down from the platform and head towards the village."

"I saw him step down, but I didn't see him go in the direction of the village. There were so many people that I couldn't see him after he stepped down."

"All right! But you got to the village before him."

"No, Your Exalted Comradeship. Nicholas was the first to get there. When I arrived at the mill, he was already dead. And you were next to his body."

"Besides you and your brother, there was no one in the village at the moment of the crime. You don't believe that the two children with scabies or Mother Anastasia could have committed the murder?"

"It wasn't the children or Mother Anastasia who killed my brother, Your Exalted Comradeship. I'm not maintaining that."

"Then it is you who killed him. No one else could have done it. Was it at the instigation of your sister-in-law that you committed this heinous fratricide? Did she bring you the knife? Was she present at the murder?"

"I did not kill my brother, Your Exalted Comradeship."

"The wife of your brother, your accomplice in this murder, has she been your mistress for a long time?"

"I have no mistress, Your Exalted Comradeship. I am a monk. I am a chaste man, a virgin..."

"That's no defense. Because you have no defense. Our Popular Republic has abolished the death penalty. Otherwise you and your wretched mistress would be put to death. The judges will condemn you to prison. For life. And before the judges, you will both confess everything, your complicity, your odious love, the fratricide... Now the citizens of the Republic will see what the hands of a monk are capable of doing, those hands they continually kiss.... The holy hands that kill and take the wife of a brother."

The interrogation of Sabina Akathist and the monk Theophorus Akathist has ended. The dossier on the murder is closed. The culpability of the accused admits of no doubt. The judges will take the floor.

Sabina and the monk are both shut up in the same cell. To humiliate them. To expose them to the mockery, crude remarks, and insults of the guards and people on the outside. It is a terrible offense to make the monk and the woman sleep in the same cell...

VII

Five Stars: The Symbol of the Secret and of Silence

THE MONK THEOPHORUS AKATHIST is confined in the same cell as Sabina, in the cellar of the Castle of the Cow. As soon as the guard locked the door, turning the key twice, Father Akathist has the terrible sensation of being deported to an unknown universe, empty and strange. He is frightened to the point of despair. The crime of fratricide he is accused of, the scandal, the injustice, and the misfortune that awaits him from now on, no longer worry him. He is at a complete loss now. For, in spite of his fifty-three years, this is the first time in his life that he finds himself enclosed in a room alone with a woman. Theophorus Akathist has never in his life come near a woman. Until the age of six and a half, he had lived with his father. Then he lived with the monks, at the monastery. His mother had died. He had never known her. He hadn't had any sisters. The feminine universe was completely foreign and unknown to him.

At the monastery, they explained to him, a monk is like salt extracted from the sea: The monk is born of a woman just as salt is drawn from the sea. But as soon as it comes into contact with water, the salt disappears, as it dissolves. At his first contact with a woman, the monk is also lost. The first commandment for a monk is to flee from women. Always and everywhere. A monk must never look at the face, or even the clothing, of a woman. If a monk is obliged to speak to a woman, something he should avoid with all his might, he must look down. He must never fix his eyes on a woman. This is not because the woman is an evil or diabolical creature. No. The woman is one of the most beautiful creatures of God. Monks are able to recognize the great excellence and beauty of women. But women belong to the world. And being a monk means first of all abandoning the world. A monk's renunciation of the world is total. This means that one gives up evil things, but also those that are good and beautiful.

When the guard locked the door of the cell, Sabina covered her face with her hands. She threw herself onto the prison bed of stone and began to moan. Father Theophorus wanted to console her. Turning his eyes towards his sister-in-law, he saw her body, stretched out on the bed, like a dress in disarray, limp. That was his first surprise. Never had he suspected that the body of a woman could be so elastic, so pliable. For the body of Sabina seemed to be without bones. It had fallen onto the bed taking on the form of sorrow and despair as a glove takes on the shape of the fingers and hand of the one who wears it. It wasn't the mouth of the woman that cried and moaned, but all her flesh. It was her hair, her arms, her back. All of it wept. This wasn't the case with men. No. The monk realized that woman is a different creation from man. It is written in the book of Genesis that God took a bone from man, from which He created woman. Man was made out of the earth. From crude material. But woman was created from matter that had already been shaped by the hand of God. It was no longer crude material. Woman was created from matter already fashioned into something superior. Perhaps that is why woman is so different. At least that's what the monk Theophorus thought.

The same sorrow which struck him and Sabina at the same time with the same force had different repercussions in each of them. Exactly like a noise made in an empty concert hall, where all the instruments of an orchestra are arranged. The same noise makes delicate instruments like the violin and lyre vibrate, almost to the point of weeping, nearly breaking their strings. But the same noise that makes sensitive strings cry out leaves the piano, trombone, and large brass instruments indifferent. Next to Sabina, who suffered lying on the bed of stone, the monk became aware of his masculine blindness, the dullness of men. He was overcome with pity. For one always has pity on those who are fragile, vulnerable, bereft of strength. Theophorus wanted to console the woman who was weeping next to him. But he didn't know how to go about it. He wanted to help her. But he didn't know how to do it. He didn't dare come any nearer. But the most amazing thing was that in spite of the fact that Sabina's entire body was covered with her clothing, so that neither her face nor legs could be seen, her body seemed naked. The woman appeared to be undressed. It was her suffering, her laments and her weeping that made her naked. And the monk didn't dare approach a naked woman. A woman who weeps, a woman who suffers and lies prostrate with grief is more naked than a woman with no clothes to cover her. All her feminine nudity is visible despite clothes. Sorrow in a woman is like an incision in her skin that reveals flesh and blood. A woman who weeps lets not only her skin, her outer nudity, be seen, but also her flesh, her blood, her entrails. With woman, suffering is interior, going to the bone. Deeper than the bone. Right to the marrow.

"Sabina, my sister, my daughter, do you want to pray with me?" asks the monk without going near her. He is ashamed of having spoken. He realizes that he is awkward and stupid. Certainly prayer is the best thing there is in the world, but perhaps this woman, at this very moment, needs something less important but more urgent. And he, a poor monk, has nothing to offer except an invitation to prayer. That is all he is able to do. Nothing else. Since the woman continues to weep, without hearing him, he says, "I'm going to pray, by myself, for you, my sister and daughter..."

The monk turns toward the east. He falls on his knees. And he says, "Maria Panagia, Maria Theotokos, Maria la Condottiera of the Not Seated, allow me to pray for this woman who is too distressed to pray herself...Theotokos, Condottiera, help her, because her sorrow rends my heart, and no one except you can assist her..."

"Father Theophorus," cries the woman, jumping out of her bed, as though bitten by a serpent, "Father Theophorus, are you here?" She looks at him, her eyes red, wide open, wild.

She sees him. She sees the monk for the first time. Until he fell on his knees facing the east, she hadn't seen him. She only saw her sorrow. He turns towards her. The woman has recovered her bones. She is angular. She has drawn back, like a scared animal, onto her bed of stone, where she had been moaning. She makes an effort to be as far as possible from the monk. She draws up her legs, lowers her chin. She has no more flesh. She is nothing but bones. To seem the least womanly that she can. He has turned towards her, and looks above her. That way he sees less of her.

"Yes, my daughter, I am here."

"Father, forgive me," says Sabina.

"May the Lord forgive you," the monk answers. He raises his right hand. Joining his fingers to make the letters of the name of Christ, he makes the sign of the cross over Sabina. He recalls that at the seminary he was told that God made the hand of man with five fingers so that he could form the name of Jesus Christ with them.

"Forgive me for not having told you the truth," she entreated him.

"God has already forgiven you, for He forgives everything."

"I know who killed Nicholas, Father..."

"Be silent for now," the priest says. "You'll tell me later. God has forgiven you in advance. Rest and get back your composure first."

Never, since he has been a priest, has the monk Theophorus felt his duty to hear confessions weigh on him so heavily. If it is a burden for a man to bear his own sins, it is incalculably more burdensome to shoulder and bear the sins of others. Especially if these others are near and dear to him. Father Theophorus is afraid and he does not want to hear Sabina's story now. He does not want to hear in detail how she took the knife and killed Nicholas. Of course, he has to hear the murderess's narrative. He is a priest. And a priest, at the last judgment, must give an account before God not only of his own sins, of his personal offenses, but especially of the offenses of his sons and daughters. A priest bears the sins of all his faithful. And he will be blamed more severely for the sins of his faithful than for his own sins. Sabina has killed her husband, but he too, the priest and spiritual father of Sabina, is guilty. Since fathers are always responsible for the crimes, sins, and faults of their children. Father Akathist wants to delay, at least for a few minutes, the terrible confession of the woman, his daughter and sister-in-law, who has murdered her husband, for the sake of a mill which no longer even belonged to them. It is an atrocious crime. Unheard of. The priest asks God for the strength to hear, calmly, as befits a priest monk—a monk and a priest—the account of the homicide. And the voice of the woman ascends from her bed of stone. The voice is enfleshed. With her voice, the woman again becomes elastic and pliable. For the monk, it is as though she were naked. He closes his eyes, but the woman transmits her softness to his ear.

"I have not had the courage to tell you, Father," Sabina continues. "Forgive me, since you are good and merciful and holy. Father, Ovid Panteleimon was the one who killed Nicholas. And I knew, wretch that I am, that he would kill him . . ."

"Who killed Nicholas?" asks the priest. "Repeat what you just said. Who killed Nicholas?"

"It was Ovid Panteleimon, Father. He is the murderer, but it was for my sake that he killed . . ."

That is a terrible revelation. Unbelievable. Among God's creatures there were already six too many in the village of the Akathists: the two children with scabies, the deaf-mute woman, the wife of the miller, the monk, and the miller himself with a knife solidly planted in his back, like a leek. And now, there would have been the poet. And the monk and the woman are still there in the cell.

Sabina's narrative breaks off suddenly, like a thread from which an overly heavy weight has been suspended.

"It's my fault, entirely," she repeats. "Nicholas, my dear Nicholas, is dead because of me, unfortunate woman that I am. It is on account of Eve, on account of a woman, that man lost paradise. And as a consequence each misfortune that crushes man comes about through the fault of a woman. Always because of a woman. And so I was the ruin of Nicholas . . ."

Father Akathist realizes that Sabina has lost her mind. She has become mad. From sorrow. What she said doesn't make any sense. Professor Ovid Panteleimon, the poet of the Condottiera, disappeared twenty years ago. He is certainly dead. And has been for quite some time. He was sentenced to the death penalty by the Muscovites several times in absentia. The Muscovites, when they plundered the country, also destroyed all that was national, authentic, Romanian, Christian. Bishops, poets, philosophers, all creative thinkers, disappeared without a trace. Exactly like Ovid Panteleimon. The Muscovites wanted to leave the herd of people without any guide, in order to put collaborators like Mavid Zeng and Caracal at their head. The intellectual leaders of the Romanian nation were exterminated. Old books were burned. When Sabina says that it was Professor Ovid Panteleimon who killed Nicholas, those are the words of a madwoman. And it isn't surprising that Sabina has become mad. During the invasion of the Muscovites, she was raped for entire days. To the point where she lost consciousness. For several weeks, she remained as though dead. Without speaking, without hearing, without seeing. But she came back to herself. And as soon as she regained consciousness, they violated her again. And then sent her to the horrific work camps, to work on the canal between the Danube and the Black Sea, where a million Romanians died. All the elite of the Romanian people were murdered at this canal, which the collaborator scribe of the Muscovites exalted in a book of a thousand pages entitled *The Road without Dust.* He is the only man in the world to sing the beauty of forced labor, the splendors of the prison camps, the loftiness of the terror wrought by the police, and the poetical charms of genocide.... After twelve years spent in this death camp, where the captives lived and died in the open air, while chained, Sabina Akathist returned to the village. But all this has left an indelible mark on her. And today, seeing herself shut up again, she loses her mind, it's normal.

"You're saying that Ovid Panteleimon is the one who killed Nicholas?" asks the priest.

"Yes, Father. He had been at the mill for more than two months..."

"Professor Ovid Panteleimon was hidden at the mill, where you live?"

"Yes, Father. You don't believe me?"

"Of course I believe you. But if he had been at the mill, I would have seen him too, Sabina. I came to your home almost every day. You're well aware of that. And I myself never saw the poet..."

"He was there, Father."

The priest is sure that she is delirious. She has lost the use of her reason. She has invented, in her deranged mind, a guilty person to clear herself of the crime she committed and that her poor conscience cannot endure. She has indicated as the guilty person the first name that came to mind. The monk is overcome with immense pity for the poor woman next to him in distress, misfortune, and the terrible sin of homicide... He does not see her. He does not even sense her presence because darkness has encompassed the cell. But from the bed of stone, though the woman is silent, her breathing continues to well up. Women exist by this kind of breathing. They don't moan in the same way men do. And now she is furious!

"You do not believe me when I say that Professor Ovid Panteleimon is the murderer of Nicholas."

"Yes, of course I do, my daughter. I believe you."

"He had been at the mill for two months," she says. "You didn't see him. You certainly never saw him. He was hidden in the old tool room, Father. You know the tool room, don't you? You remember it. It is the small storage area beside our bedroom upstairs, right above the millstones.... Nicholas set up Panteleimon's bed up there. He never left his hiding place. You never noticed that the door to the old tool room was always shut?"

"I believe you, my dear Sabina. Of course I believe you. From the moment you told me that. But if the professor had been hidden in our home, at the mill, I would have been aware of it. I would have known. I would have seen him. Nicholas would have told me he was there. The professor would have spoken to me too."

"The professor forbade us to tell you. He said that if the police found him and if they executed all three of us, that would be enough. There was no need for a fourth death. And above all he didn't want you, a priest, to lose your life on his account. He used to say that priests were the lieutenants of the Condottiera, the only guides of the Romanian people in these unfortunate times. Priests must be spared. He forbade us to tell you he was there, hidden. He suffered terribly in his hiding place. Since he wanted to go to confession and receive communion. But he didn't want to expose you to death. He asked us to bring him, every Sunday, a piece of the *antidoron*, the blessed bread. You never noticed that I always asked you for an extra *antidoron* after the liturgy? It was for him. But he killed my husband.... The criminal!"

Sabina weeps. The monk cannot believe this story. He thinks of the salt drawn from the sea. At its first contact with water, the salt dissolves. The monk is at the other end of the cell, in the corner opposite the woman. But, during the night which has consumed all the shadows, he knows she is there, her chin on her knees, curled up, as though closed in. He should distrust her. The first commandment for a monk is to flee from woman. And this one is insistent. She doesn't avoid contact, even if she is at a distance, all bones, invisible. No, the woman persists in trying to convince him. That is where there is contact. Theophorus realizes that he is trembling as he hears Sabina's voice.

"You still don't believe me? I swear to you that it's true. He had been with us for two months. And he is the one who killed Nicholas. With the knife that was on the table. When Nicholas got back from the festivities. They were alone at the mill..."

"Ovid Panteleimon had no reason to kill Nicholas.

Supposing he was at the mill, he would have felt nothing but gratitude. Because Nicholas was hiding him. And then, he always loved Nicholas, from the first day they met. He came to the village, even though he was a minister, to be best man at your wedding.... It's absurd to say that Ovid Panteleimon killed Nicholas. Besides, my dear Sabina, poor Ovid Panteleimon must have been dead for twenty years now.... The collaborators didn't allow him to live. He was too great a poet and he loved Romania too much to be pardoned by the invaders and their collaborators."

"You think I'm crazy, Father?" asks Sabina. She was desperate. "I'm telling you the truth and you're looking at me as though I were delirious. That's not fair, Father! Do you really think I'm mad?"

"Certainly not mad. But you're crushed with sorrow. Sorrow is worse than alcohol. Sorrow takes away your reason. It makes your mind delusional. Saying no matter what. Sorrow is more powerful than brandy..."

"So you don't believe me when I say that Ovid Panteleimon was at the mill and that he killed Nicholas?"

"It has been twenty years since the poet Panteleimon disappeared, my dear Sabina.... The collaborators searched even the bowels of the earth, and killed all those of merit. They couldn't have missed Ovid Panteleimon. For them, he was more dangerous than a whole army. They say that if you put on one side of a scale all the people, and on the other side the soul of the national poet, the soul of the poet would weigh more than all his people. The Muscovites couldn't let him live. They killed him. He is dead. So then he couldn't have been hidden at the mill. He couldn't have killed Nicholas. Rest a while and later you can make your confession. Because God forgives everything. Everything."

"You're talking like the militia, Father," says Sabina, weeping. "You refuse to believe me, Father..."

The woman falls on her knees. The monk does not turn his head toward the bundle of a woman, nothing but clothes, an undefined mass, entreating. Her supplication is like the sea. All the salt of the earth could dissolve there in the devastating ocean, the maternal sea. The virgin of the Not Seated, the Condottiera, is herself a mass of feelings, of compassion. The monk is bent on seeing and hearing only this unique woman, all roundness, all softness, who becomes a sheltering conch for the Infant-God. And he again finds in himself unsullied compassion for Sabina. Unsullied and focused, because salt must always beware of water, though pure.

"I believe you. Because you affirm it. You're saying then that Professor Ovid Panteleimon had been hidden at the mill for two months. In the old storage room for tools. Over the millstones. And that you kept his presence hidden from me in order not to expose me to death, is that right?"

"That's it exactly.... We didn't want to tell you he was there. He kept telling us, 'if they find me here, all three of us will be shot. Three people would then die. But if a priest dies too, then God dies with him. Not just a man. A priest is the bearer of the Holy Spirit. A priest deifies the world. And if a priest is killed, it's a deifier who dies, in this time of blasphemy, sacrilege, and misfortune. When only sanctification and deification can keep us alive, supernaturally... Since historically, we have been given over to extermination.... The life of Father Akathist must be spared. You must hide from him the fact that I'm at the mill. In sparing the priest, God is spared. And God is preserved in the country of the Akathists, in the land of Vrancea. As long as the priest is here, God is present here. Among us. And we can have every hope. And courage. In spite of the millions of Muscovite soldiers who have occupied our land and have been killing us for twenty years with the bloody hands of the Party of Collaborators...' That's what he said to me and to Nicholas, each time he saw you at the mill."

"And he is the one who killed Nicholas?"

"Yes, Father. He is the one. Because of me..."

Slowly, very slowly, stopping from time to time to cry, Sabina tells how, two months before, during the night, around three o'clock in the morning, they heard the door of the mill open. Then steps going up the staircase. Then they saw the door open, the door of the bedroom where Nicholas and his wife slept.

"Be still. Stay where you are and don't make any noise," ordered the man who entered the miller's bedroom. Sabina was huddled next to her husband. They were terribly afraid. Outside it was dark. Rain was falling in torrents. The man who came into their bedroom carried a sack on his head to protect himself from the rain. They saw the outline of his frightening silhouette in the dark. But what was even more awful was his odor. As soon as he entered, closing the door noiselessly behind him, the room was filled with the odor of a wet sack, of moldy straw, of manure, and of a hunted animal.... They suffocated. They felt that if the door was not opened soon enough, they would faint.

The man was standing in front of the door. And it was from him, from his dark, frightening shadow, that these odors from hell emanated. Odors like that of game, especially stags and deer, when they drop dead, not from bullets, but from fatigue, from fear, when they have been tracked down for too long.

"Don't make any noise, Nicholas Akathist. Don't turn on the light. I am Ovid Panteleimon.... The poet of the Condottiera. Or, more exactly, I'm what's left of the poet Ovid Panteleimon..."

As he said these words, Professor Panteliemon sat down on the floor in front of the door. Right where he was. He slid down in a state of collapse, his body in the shape of a coat fallen to the floor, not having been hung up properly. They heard the water dripping from his rags. They smelled the sweat running down his skin. He wasn't what could be called sitting. No. He had fallen, like something wet falls off the coat rack. He was dead tired.

"I know, dear millers, my dear Akathists, that what I'm bringing you tonight in coming to your house is death. If they find me, then you, Nicholas, and you, Sabina, will be shot on the spot. Without a trial. By the militia. For the crime of allowing me to enter. Everyone who gives shelter to the poet Ovid Panteleimon will be shot at once. Poets are the most formidable witnesses to the foreign occupation. For that reason they are killed. But I myself am still living. It is the Condottiera, the Theotokos, the Mother of God, who has kept me alive. Miraculously, as only the Panagia can do. For twenty years, from August 23, 1944, the day of the occupation and of the creation of the Penitentiary Republic of Romania, I have lived in a closet. In the center of Bucharest. A few steps from the old royal palace. For twenty years, I hoped to leave the closet and escape to the West. But, the days passed, and I stayed in my cubbyhole. A closet a little bigger than a coffin. A few weeks ago, the militia expelled all the occupants of the building. They sent bulldozers, and leveled the entire block of buildings. And my closet as well. I had to leave. The person who had hidden me lived in an apartment where there was no closet for me. And so I ran outside, like rats do when a ship is burning. I ran towards the west. Like the sun. But the sun courses to the west during the day. I had to run at night, hoping that in the West I'd be able to sit down. Lie down. Sleep.

"I tried all the methods of escape I had dreamed of for twenty years. But if one can escape from the most formidable prisons every once in a while, it is impossible to flee from the Penitentiary Republic. I was too old, of course. If I had been younger, I would have succeeded. When I was thwarted, I had to retrace my steps. I wandered in the mountains. And I remembered, when I came to the land of Vrancea, that that's where the mill of the Condottiera is located. I kept watch. I saw that you were both alive. You, Nicholas, and you, Sabina, whose wedding I witnessed. And I have come to bring you death. You, in return, can give me life, by taking me in. Each gives what he has. And what he is able to. The exchange isn't fair. Since I bring you death and you give me life. That's no exchange to propose to merchants. But it's an exchange that we Christians have made, following the example of Christ. For two thousand years. Do you accept death to give me life?"

There was silence.

"I can no longer walk. If you do not accept the death that my presence may bring you, notify the militia. I'll have enough strength to go down to the middle of the road, so I won't be killed here, in the mill.... I could not walk any further..."

As they listen, the tears of Nicholas and Sabina fall onto their pillows, without their being aware of it. "Of course we accepted the exchange proposed by the poet. Because we are Christians. That's the only thing left to us. And we accepted death, to give life to the poet. And every day, we waited for the payment to fall due. Every morning, when Nicholas and I woke up, we prepared to be shot during the day. Every evening, when we went to bed, we prepared to be awakened during the night and to be shot. As the poet could be discovered at any moment. It was a miracle he wasn't. All day long, the mill is full of people who look all around them, whose gaze penetrates everywhere. And the professor was hidden right above their heads. But no one discovered him. Misfortune had to come from elsewhere. As it always does. Since true misfortune comes from inside, from ourselves. Not from outside."

Sabina stops. The monk can bear the silence at last. The story of the crime has removed the woman from the cell. Within its four walls, there is only the crime and the monk.

"What happened?" he asks.

"I'm ashamed to say, Father Theophorus. Very ashamed. Because it was my fault. And I knew, from the moment the poet came, that the drama would detonate. Nicholas told him to stay at the mill, to make himself at home, that the risk was of no account when we were willing to give our lives to save a poet. Because a poet is the homeland itself. Then the professor said:

"'Maybe Sabina, your wife, whom the Panagia Condottiera gave you, in the midst of the waters, along with the mill, will go in your place to inform the militia. Since she may not want to die! ...'

"'I would not commit such a crime, Professor,' I said. On hearing my voice, the professor smiled. We were in darkness. We could barely see the shape of his head, covered with a sack, his shaggy, bushy beard, his broad shoulders.... And as soon as he smiled, we saw his face. His smile was luminous, Father. His smile was as though phosphorescent. I never knew up until that moment that if a man smiles with his whole heart, in the dark, his smile shines like a light. I didn't know before this that the happiness of a man is luminous. That it can be seen even in the dark. And I saw with my eyes that his smile was really a light. All smiles and all happiness shine like gold and precious gems in the dark, in the shadows. Of course, the whiteness of teeth also makes a smile light up in the dark. But with the poet, who was happy when he smiled, it wasn't his teeth that were bright. His whole head glowed with light. Like the head of a saint, surrounded by a halo. I understood that he was happy, not so much because he had found a refuge with us, at the mill, but because he had heard my voice, the voice of a woman. He acknowledged this himself, as he said,

"'How sweet it is to hear, so close to my ear, the voice of a woman.... Of a young woman. There's nothing sweeter on earth than the voice of a woman.... No music equals it. For twenty years, in my closet, I didn't hear a feminine voice a single time.... And that was the hardest thing about all my captivity in the closet...'

"'You can stay, Professor,' Nicholas said. And with his practical bent, he arranged everything. At daybreak Ovid Panteleimon had his hiding place. He had washed, shaved, and put on clean clothes, Nicholas's clothes.

"'Is your holy brother, the priest monk Theophorus, still alive?' the professor asked.

"'He spent a dozen years in prison, like all Romanians. He left at the same time as Sabina. In 1956, when the men of the Carpathians and the birds of China were amnestied. When they were allowed to keep on living. Since his monastery was closed, he came to the village. He is our parish priest, our confessor. We're one of the few villages that still have a priest. A priest who believes in God, since in other villages they installed collaborators dressed in a cassock at the churches. Who talk about the miracles of the Muscovites, the miracles of Mavid Zeng and of their Party. In theory, our father and brother Theophorus lives at the mill. But in fact he's never here. He continues to celebrate the monastic services at the church, with the liturgy every day, the night offices, and continual prayer. He only comes to the mill now and then, to wash his shirt and take a little food. He is an *acoemetic* monk, who hardly ever sleeps, so as not to interrupt his prayer. When he wants to sleep, he sits down in a chair, in the middle of the church, his face towards the altar, and falls asleep as he recites the *Psalterion*, and saying, until he can no longer move his lips, "Lord Jesus Christ, have mercy on me, a poor sinner!..." He says that to the rhythm of his heartbeats. And when he can no longer move his lips, when he falls asleep, his heart continues to say the same phrase with each beat. He says that monks have the duty to never interrupt their prayers, during the time when the faithful can no longer pray. That monks must pray in place of all the people who are under the yoke of foreigners and no longer have the right to pray.'

"'The holy father Theophorus must not be told that I'm here...,' Ovid Panteleimon said. 'His life must not be endangered. Because if they shoot him, the continual prayers of our people will be interrupted. And the line of prayer that unites us to heaven must not be broken. Ever. This link is our only chance for hope and salvation.'"

Sabina weeps. Her tears are the sea. The monk is once more alone with her. He closes his eyes. The voice of the woman enters into him to dissolve him. In the name of charity. In the name of God.

"Now you see, Father, why we didn't want to reveal to you that Ovid Panteleimon was hidden in our mill. It was to keep God in our village, by keeping you alive."

"What did he do all day in his hiding place? Did he write or read?"

"Never," Sabina replies. "The hiding place was so small that he could only fit into it by lying down. Nicholas tried to get him to leave from time to time. But he refused. He said that after the twenty years he had spent in a closet, it seemed to him that his life could not run its normal course unless he was stretched out like a dead man in his coffin. I think he prayed. He prayed all the time. He called himself the poet of the

Condottiera. Once in a while he spoke to us about his plans to escape to the West. But after the attempts he had made, which failed, he no longer had the courage to try. He was very tired. He was too tired even to dream. Only when I came near him or when I spoke to him did his face light up. Panteleimon was becoming handsome. He was regaining courage, and hope. He became intelligent and brilliant again, as in the past. Because the rest of the time he wouldn't have been said to be the most brilliant poet and an eminent professor. His mind had been deadened. He had been reduced to a vegetal state. When I saw that he became himself again as soon as he saw me or felt my presence, near his hiding place, then I understood that he was in love with me. I told that to Nicholas. He laughed. He said that Ovid Panteleimon was an old man, that he was only a shadow of what he had been. But, several times, when I brought his food to the hiding place, he touched my hand, with fear, but it was an unequivocal gesture. Then my hip. I pretended not to notice it. I let him do it. It was as though I was letting a child play. Seeing that this was restoring happiness to him, his only happiness and seeing that it was pure, without any sin, I let him do it. But then he began to look at me in such a way that I felt his eyes on my skin, my hips, my breasts, like moist snails climbing up my skin. He looked at me so insistently that I felt his gaze physically, like serpents which crept under my dress, under my slip, going up my body. I couldn't stand it any more. I avoided going to take him his food. Nicholas did it instead. That's when he began to suffer."

The cell is like the beach when the tide is coming in. Each grain of salt, long in advance, feels the proximity of the water. By the time the waves break, inundating the salt, absorbing it, it has already experienced its sweet agony for a long time. The monk becomes a molecule of salt again. With his facets and angles, he asks, almost like a judge, "Did he say anything?"

"Nothing. But he was offended. He knew that I had spoken to my husband. He was humiliated. He was saddened to the depths of his soul. I had pity on him. I began to bring him his food again. Now he no longer looked at me. He hated me. All his love had turned into hate. Like the choicest wine becomes vinegar. He suffered atrociously. He particularly hated Nicholas. More than me. Because it was in the eyes of my miller that he had been humiliated and abased, as a man. When I spoke to Nicholas, that meant that I preferred my husband to him. And it was unquestionable that the only obstacle between him and me was my husband. He became gloomy. His expression revealed his criminal plan. I told Nicholas that the professor wanted to kill him. But Nicholas laughed. I explained to him that poets are generally irritable, complicated people. And after twenty years of life in a closet, anything could be expected from a poet. They are really crazy. I told Nicholas to hide the knife that was on the table. Because I feared for his life . . . . And I wasn't spared from what I had feared so much. August 23, when Nicholas got back, the professor left with him to go on a walk by the mill, since there was no one in the village to see him, and then he killed him. To get revenge for his humiliation. In an act of madness. Because he wasn't completely normal. Of course, poets are never normal human beings. They're always a little crazy. But if you keep them shut up in a closet for twenty years, then their madness reaches full bloom. And Ovid Panteleimon was insane and he killed my husband . . . "

"You did not see him commit the murder with your own eyes?" the priest says.

With the murder of Nicholas Akathist, the sea began to subside.

"The knife was on the table. He was the only one who could take it and stick it between Nicholas's shoulders.... I had felt for a long time that he would do it. For days and days I was certain that he would come at night and kill Nicholas with the knife that was on the table.... I am a woman, Father, and I sense, without needing to see or be in contact with what's happening around me, what is in the minds and hearts of the people near me.... Ovid Panteleimon had wanted to kill Nicholas for a long time. He was only waiting for an opportunity. And he had his opportunity on August 23, when he was alone with Nicholas in the village..."

"He also could have been angry at Nicholas because he gave the mill to the collaborators."

"No. He said that was a matter he had no opinion about. Because he used to say that he was dead. And the dead have no opinion about the things of this world. He had no opinions. About anything."

Everything Sabina related to Father Akathist was true. There are tones of voice that cannot be mistaken. And because all that was true, a long silence ensued. A terrible silence.

"He killed Nicholas. But no one can condemn him, Father. No one. He wasn't himself. Twenty years in a closet, Father. And you want a man to go out and behave normally after all that? No. He is not blameworthy. In spite of his crime. Besides, the guilty one is me. Because I provoked his hatred of Nicholas. And his jealousy of Nicholas. It was me, it was my presence. I was his temptation. This accursed flesh of a woman. It is the true criminal. The perpetrator of the murder was my flesh."

"You have nothing to reproach yourself with," the priest says.

"Yes I do, Father. My presence was enough. It is to prevent such crimes that sailors forbid women from getting aboard their warships. And that monks do not permit any women to set foot in their monastic space ... "

Sabina strikes her breast with her fists, with force. The monk hears the blows. But beneath these blows, the woman is now without bones. The sweetness which receives the blows dilutes away the violence which strikes. And the woman speaks. She wants to exorcise all her sweetness. She wants to hide all her weakness. And here she is nothing but sweetness, nothing but weakness.

"Even at my age and after so much suffering and after twelve years in prison, with my wrinkles and white hair, I continue to be a temptation, the instigator of a crime, an occasion of ruin .... Cursed be my woman's flesh ... "

She continues to weep. Then she gets up abruptly and says, "Father, what can we do now? Tell me, what can we do? We're both left to be condemned for a heinous crime which we did not commit. Or should we tell the truth instead? It is easy to declare that Ovid Panteleimon is the killer. His fingerprints must be on the knife. His bed, his hiding place, traces of him, all this is still at the mill. Even if he fled after the murder. The militia can confirm this. And come to the conclusion that he is the one that killed my miller. That it wasn't you. And that it wasn't me." Sabina falls to her knees once again. Exhausted, battered.

"If we declare that we're innocent of the crime they're charging us with, and that we gave shelter to the poet Ovid Panteleimon, instead of sending us to prison for the rest of our lives, they'll shoot us on the spot. For killing a man you're sentenced to forced labor for life. But for giving refuge to the greatest Romanian poet, one who only committed a single crime, that of loving his people and his country, we will immediately be given the death penalty, without a trial. It is an unpardonable crime, and the biggest one in the eyes of the occupiers and collaborators."

"We'll let them convict us, in spite of our innocence?"

"Since we're not guilty, we have to choose the lesser penalty. We will keep our secret. We will not say that Ovid Panteleimon is the killer. In order to save our lives, and then we'll entrust them to Maria, la Condottiera."

"I don't want to go to prison, Father"

"You only have a choice between prison and death. We will choose prison. Because we're Christians. And we know that as long as we have life and keep ourselves pure, Maria, la Condottiera, our protector, will not forget us. We'll say nothing about Ovid Panteleimon. Absolutely nothing."

On the beach, the sea has receded, into infinity. The sand had found peace again. The monk has regained the star. The star is called certitude. It shines in the darkness of the cell. It illuminates. It dazzles. It restores to the woman the form of her figure and the realization of the immensity of her distress, of her desolation. The path to prison opens before the monk and the woman. But prison is nothing. Prison is from man. And man cannot prevail against the star.

"Between ourselves, the symbol is: *Five stars*. That's the cipher of the secret. And of silence. It is used by icon painters in the West. It has a very beautiful history. In the Middle Ages, in Prague, there was a priest named John Nepomucene. He was confessor to the queen. The king, who was jealous, asked the priest confessor if the queen had told him that she had a lover and was deceiving her husband. The priest did not break the seal of confession. For that reason, he was killed and thrown from the top of a bridge into the waters of the Moldau. He died as a martyr. Painters wrote on his icon the word *TACUI*, 'I kept silent.' Then those five letters on the icon of the holy martyr were replaced by five stars. Stars are more beautiful than letters. And from that time, five stars have represented, in iconography, silence and the secret of confession. Our symbol from now on will be five stars. We will keep silent. We will not divulge the name of the one who killed Nicholas. God will judge him. As for ourselves, we'll accept the fate that God will permit the invaders of our country and their collaborators to reserve for us. But Sabina, since we're Christians, we're optimists. For we have the faith. And confidence in our God. As St. Paul says: 'Faith is the assurance of things hoped for.'"

Sabina smiles. She is thinking of the five stars. And of the Condottiera, the Mother of God, whose standard will be emblazoned with five stars from now on.

VIII

The Transfer

A WEEK HAS PASSED SINCE THE MURder of the miller Nicholas Akathist. The police investigation has been completed. The file is closed. The two accused, the monk Theophorus and his sister-in-law Sabina, are in prison, at the Castel Vaca. They are awaiting their trial and sentencing. The trial will take place in the main square of the town. They will be judged by a tribunal of the people. A platform will be erected, like the one for the parade of August 23. Thousands and thousands of people will attend the trial of the monk who killed his brother to take his wife. No one will dare to testify on behalf of the two criminals. Their deed is too monstrous. They have no excuses, neither on earth nor in heaven. After being shut away together, the accused were separated. Each is chained to the cell wall. At night, the monk Theophorus hears the moans and tears of Sabina. She is confined in a cell in the same corridor as the monk's, and close enough for him to hear her cries and laments during the night, but too far for him to be able to talk to her. Between the woman and the monk, there is only the thickness of a wall. The voice of the woman penetrates this wall. The monk hears her, but her words are distorted, unclear. A voice that would seem to be clothed, a voice out on a visit. It evokes compassion on the part of the monk, but it has lost the spellbinding agitation of the sea. The voice of Sabina is nothing more than the voice of misfortune. And misfortune has no sex. The nights of the monk Theophorus are filled with the voice of misfortune. He waits. He is like dust blown away by the wind. He is going to be tried, with his sister-in-law, for fratricide. They will be hauled up onto the platform in front of the crowd gathered there. They will be accused of murder and fornication. They will be condemned to prison. The monk has no fear of prison. There is imprisonment on this earth only for those who have lost the faith. Theophorus contemplates the cry let out by the woman, "I don't want to go back to prison!" No doubt that is what she is crying out, at night, turning over on the bed of stone in her cell, a bundle of flesh wet with tears. Each night the woman weeps. The monk prays.

August 29, day of the beheading of the holy and illustrious prophet and precursor John the Baptist, around two o'clock in the afternoon the doors of the two cells were opened, and the monk and the woman were ordered to leave.

"Follow me quickly," commanded Zid Caracal. Guards flanking the prisoners pushed them out.

In front of the Castle of the Cow, a black car was waiting, with two men in civilian dress.

"Get into the car, hurry up," ordered Caracal, bustling about. The two men in civilian clothes were certainly persons of rank. From the capitol. Caracal was servile towards them. There was no end to his bowing and his use of the title "Your Exalted Comradeship."

In the car, the priest and the woman were pushed into the back seat. They had taken nothing with them. The two men in civilian dress — two important members of the militia, very elegant — got in front. Before they started up the car, Zid Caracal bowed before them, with a register in his hand.

"Sign this receipt for me," Caracal requested.

The policeman at the wheel signed, without taking off his glove.

"You'll bring them back to us, Your Exalted Comradeship?"

"This is a permanent transfer," he said.

Zid Caracal's face clouded over, suddenly. The cruel giant, the iron spear of the militia in the land of Vrancea, the right hand of Mavid Zeng, grew pale. He even staggered. It did not please him at all that they were taking the two prisoners from him. And that they wouldn't be bringing them back. The two men in civilian dress noticed that Zid Caracal was agitated.

"You're not happy to be rid of them?" asked the policeman who had signed the receipt.

The car took off abruptly. They sped down the hill, went through the village of the Akathists, passing by the church and the mill, then headed south. The prisoners hardly had a few seconds to look at their village. They knew with certainly that was the last time they would see it. The priest made the sign of the cross. It was the beginning of his longest trip. Which would end in death. The two militiamen in civilian clothes smelled of cologne and brilliantine, and they smoked fragrant American cigarettes. They consulted their watches nervously. They didn't cast a glance at the prisoners in the back seat. It was as though they didn't exist. They were there like parcels.

"Where are they taking us, Father?" Sabina asked. She was in anguish.

During a week of captivity, they had gotten used to the idea of being tried, booed by the people, having stones thrown at them, and then being sentenced and cast into the depths of a prison, in heavy chains. And all of a sudden, things were happening otherwise. They were taken away in a fine car. They weren't in chains. They weren't flanked by militia with bayonets aimed at them. No one insulted them. No one beat them. When Sabina spoke to the priest, asking where they were being transferred, the policeman did not strike her and order her to be quiet. They did not even listen to what she was saying to her fellow prisoner. But a prisoner must never trust appearances. When jailers smile at captives and offer them cigarettes, it is precisely because they want to shoot them. Sabina and the Akathist priest knew all that.

"Do you think they're going to shoot us without a trial?" Sabina asks.

"Let's be ready for anything, my daughter!"

"At the canal, when the militia from the outside brought someone there, it was always to execute him. He was never seen again . . ."

The woman weeps. The militiamen notice her in the rear view mirror. But they remain indifferent.

The priest monk Theophorus Akathist does not want to frighten Sabina further. For that reason, he is silent. But he thinks he understands the abrupt change that has occurred. The militia have certainly arrested Professor Ovid Panteleimon. He must have admitted that he killed the miller. Now they are going to bring them face to face with Panteleimon. That's why they have taken them away. They did not put them in chains, they did not put guards on either side of them, and they are letting them talk. Because now the militia know that they are not the murderers of the miller Nicholas. It is always the justice of God that brings the truth to light.

Suddenly the priest becomes sad. Because if they are cleared of the charge of murder, their punishment will be worse. They would not be tried in public and sentenced to forced labor for life for the crime of fratricide and murder. They would be shot without a trial. By administrative decision. For having sheltered and hidden the poet Ovid Panteleimon. That is a more serious crime than homicide.

The policemen have turned on the radio. There is languid music playing. They are now driving across the plain. It is the fertile plain the Akathists, the Not Seated, have gone down to for generations each spring, to work the land of others during the warm weather. The villages are empty. The harvests are abundant, ripe, golden. The monk Theophorus has a sense of well-being. Because the plain is fertile. And fertile soil is a feast for the eyes, as gratifying to look at as velvet and silk. Theophorus is proud of the fruitfulness of the Romanian earth. It is the soil of his homeland. It is an extension of his physical being. Of his own flesh. Flesh that will rise again at the last judgment. At the apocatastasis. Then, not only will the flesh and bones of men be resurrected, but also the earth, trees, all the cosmos that man has sanctified and deified by his life. All the Romanian land will come back to life on the day of the great judgment.

Before August 23, 1944 Romania was a country with a round border, like the moon and the sun. After the invasion and occupation, they seized and annexed the provinces of Bessarabia, Bucovina, and part of Dobrogea to the Muscovite empire. The country is now mutilated. Physically, as well as spiritually. Their freedom has been taken away. Their rights have been abolished. They are in chains. And the border has been amputated. On the map as well as in history, Romania is severely mutilated. A disabled, wounded country. And kept captive. In chains. To add to the humiliation, sorrow, and suffering of the land and of the people, they even changed the name of the country. They disfigured it by prohibiting the spelling "Romania." It is the only country in the world that has kept the name of its Roman origin. It is really that which has been prohibited. It is forbidden under penalty of imprisonment to write "Romania." It must be spelled "Rominia," with an "i." To suppress the visible sign of the Roman origin of Romanians. So that no one will be aware that "Romans" and "Romanians" are the same word, designating those descended from Rome.

Suddenly the car comes to a stop. They are in a big city. A city on the plain. They are in the center of town. In front of the biggest building. A palace. It could be, in normal times, the city hall. Now, under the occupation of 1944, the biggest building of a town is not the city hall, but the seat of the militia and the PC, the Party of Collaborators with the occupier.

"Out!" cries the elegant militiaman at the wheel. He turns off the radio. Father Akathist and Sabina try to open the doors. But they stay closed. They do not know how to go about this. It's the first time in their lives that they've been in a passenger car.

"Get out, you two!" the militiaman cries. "You don't understand Romanian?" He doesn't take the trouble to note that the monk and the woman do not know how to open the doors. For them, for the collaborators with the occupier, who spend a lot of time in cars, such a hypothesis is not considered.

The two guards on duty in front of the monumental building come running. They open the doors. Sabina and the monk get out.

"Get going, get going, damn it," the militiaman shouts. They push the captives onto a great stone staircase. The militiamen in civilian clothes follow them. The two guards as well. They run up the stairs. They are in a big hurry.

"Take them to the warehouse right away. These are the people with scabies they telephoned about from the Supreme Presidium, this morning. Have them dressed quickly. In five minutes, they should be ready."

The militiaman who is at the entrance bows to show that he has understood.

"I have received the order concerning them. We were waiting for you. All the finery is ready..."

They push the woman and the monk through the vast marble hall. Then down a long corridor. In front of all the doors there are orderlies, silent, holding fixed bayonets. No one speaks. No one moves. Except the militiamen pushing the two captives from behind. Without violence. But with haste. Father Akathist and Sabina have heard the word "scabies." They understood that it applied to them. Then the militiamen said that someone from the Supreme Presidium had made a phone call concerning them. In the language of the Muscovites, the Presidium is the equivalent of the Imperial Palace. This must be very serious. Then they talked about finery. That's slang. That might mean that they're going to put chains on them, handcuffs. Since that's what prisoners wear. Maybe the centurions used a similar word, adornment, in giving the order for the crown of thorns to be placed on Christ.

"Wait here," the militiaman orders. He knocks at a door, which is opened. "Here are the two people with scabies, sent by the Supreme Presidium. You must quickly dress them up. The car is waiting outside..."

Father Theophorus is now certain that Ovid Panteleimon has been arrested. And that they will be brought face to face with him at the Supreme Presidium, at the Imperial Palace of the Occupiers, before very important persons. That is the reason for their hurried transfer.

"Come in, come in," shouts the adjutant, opening the door. He is wearing a white smock. Sabina and the monk are shoved inside. It's a big room with very high ceilings, and aisles, with clothes racks, as in a department store, displaying thousands and thousands of suits, gowns, dresses, uniforms, top hats.... An odor of disinfectant is prevalent.

"What is your size, monk?" asks the head of the clothing warehouse. "And you, woman, what is your size?"

Neither the priest nor the woman knows their

size. They have never had their measurements taken. There was no reason for this. Of what use would it be, in a monastery, to know the height of one's body in centimeters?

"These people are from the Middle Ages," the militiaman says with scorn.

For twenty years, the Muscovite invaders have told the Romanians that in occupying their country, they have made them leave the Middle Ages and have civilized them. That they brought asphalt roads and electricity to Romania. Even public housing was presented as a miracle accomplished by the Muscovites in the occupied country. It is exactly as though the president of the French Republic claimed, in 1964, to be greater than St. Louis, because under his presidency the Champs-Élysées was illuminated with electric lights and the French had television sets. The way of life of the whole planet has changed. The Muscovite invaders can take no credit for this. While the collaborators of the Muscovites built several kilometers of asphalt roads for their own use, to roll along in their cars, and while they constructed some factories in the fettered country, the cannibals of Africa came down from their tree-top dwellings to move into concrete houses supplied with running water and electricity. Without being occupied by the Muscovites. The whole planet has made progress. And progress is the exclusive work of the free countries of the West, which have generously brought it to the whole world, to the Indians just as to the Muscovites and black people. Since the world has existed, the only works foreign invaders have wrought in putting peoples in chains and reducing them to slavery are tears and curses. Such are the accomplishments of every occupation and the projects of all collaboration with the foreign occupier. Never any progress. Since where people do not have freedom, there is no progress.

"There is no time for custom-made clothes for him, Comrade," the militiaman says. "Give him something we have in stock, a cassock. And let the woman herself select the coat and dress that suit her. And above all, do it quickly. In five minutes they should be on their way... "

Father Theophorus Akathist is led to an aisle where there are dozens and dozens of cassocks and black clerical suits hanging on clothes racks. There are shelves with numberless head coverings of priests, monks, bishops. One would think he was in the vestiary of a great ecumenical council. This impression would not be false. For the priests, metropolitans, deacons, and bishops, whose *anterions*, head coverings, and cloaks have been deposited here, are assembled in the holiest of synods, in heaven, where they went as martyrs. In this warehouse of the militia are piled the vestments of those who were murdered for refusing to bend the knee before the invaders and their henchmen.

"What are you waiting for, monk?" the warehouse manager cries. "Take something you like, and get dressed fast. This is at the Party's expense.... This doesn't often happen to monks!"

As Father Akathist hesitates, the manager throws him a silk *anterion*. The face of the priest clouds over. For this is the vestment of a bishop who died for his faith.

"You don't want to try it on?"

"This is the *anterion* of a bishop," the priest replies. "I am only a priest."

"Find yourself something else!" the manager orders.

A few meters behind him, in another aisle, where women's clothes are located, Sabina starts to weep and lament. She too does not dare make a selection. Like Father Akathist, she spent twelve years in forced labor. She knows the provenance of these clothes. It is as though they had price tags of blood. These are the garments of Romanians killed by the Muscovites and especially by the collaborators. Before throwing the corpses of prisoners in a common grave, they undressed them and buried them naked. To wear these clothes, one must have courage.

The manager and the militiaman choose for them. The priest puts on a cassock he has been given. He leaves his behind. It is worn out, torn. Sabina puts on a black coat. They give her a handbag. Then pushing them, very hard now, because they are late, they take them to the car that is waiting for them. The two militiamen are in front. The radio of the car is turned on. They do not even look at the prisoners. They do not care whether they are dressed or naked. When the guard closes the rear doors, the car leaves. At full speed. As soon as she's once again beside Father Akathist, Sabina clings to him, her fingers like claws.

"Where are they taking us, Father?"

Neither dares look at the other. So as not to see the martyrs' clothes they have been given. They are committing a sacrilege by wearing relics of martyrs.

"Why have they dressed us up?"

"They have undoubtedly arrested Ovid Panteleimon. They're taking us to Bucharest. For a confrontation between us and him."

"Should we still deny that he was hidden at the mill?" Sabina asks.

"It is too late to deny it. We will tell the truth."

"They're going to shoot us, Father."

"Have confidence in the Condottiera of the Akathists," says the priest. "We have to die one day or another. We must not be too frightened."

The prisoners are silent. They have nothing more to ask each other. Nothing more to say. It is really time for the Condottiera, the Mother of God, to speak. Only she can bring about a change in things. For this reason, instead of crying and asking the priest whatever comes into her head, Sabina imitates Theophorus. She prays like him, saying "Lord Jesus Christ, have mercy on me."

After a few hours on the road, in the evening, when the sun sets in the west, they arrive at the capitol. It is not yet night. But the lights of Bucharest are lit. Like stars. Neither the monk nor Sabina has ever visited the capital. But they won't see any more of it. Because on reaching the suburbs of Bucharest, the car turns to the left. Instead of heading towards the center of town, they cross districts where there are factories and barracks, going down dingy, badly-lit streets.

They think they are being taken to one of the fortresses which are always located outside the city. That is where they lock up big criminals. Those of the stature of Ovid Panteleimon, who committed the greatest crime there is, that of loving his people and his country.

"We're leaving the city," Sabina says.

The car travels away from the suburbs, on byways. There are no houses on either side of the road. Nor barracks. Nor factories. In their stead, barbed wire. And a notice, "Military territory."

"This is the army's shooting range," thinks the priest. He is certain they will be shot that evening. At night they will be in heaven. Otherwise, they would not have been brought there. Outside the city walls. So they can be executed. Because in spite of the changes wrought by men for the past two thousand years, executions are still carried out outside the city. As in the time of Christ.

"This is where we're going to die. To the east of Bucharest," the priest thinks.

"If they wanted to kill us, Father, why have they dressed us in such fine clothes?" asks Sabina.

"They're going to film our execution," the priest says. "I don't see any other reason. It's because we won't be executed secretly that they have dressed us up. We're entitled to a public execution. In front of television and movie cameras, photographers and journalists." The priest knows that Christ was also obliged to change His clothes before being taken outside the city and executed. They gave Him a red robe. They even placed a crown of thorns on His brow. To him, the miserable monk Theophorus Akathist, they have given a fine cassock, which had belonged to a holy martyr and confessor. It is a garment more glorious than the cloak of a king.

The priest monk is already used to the idea of dying. He no longer suffers. What bothers him terribly is that he will be shot in public. In front of floodlights and journalists. There is no doubt. They were given the clothes on account of the cameras. The thought of dying in public makes Father Theophorus ill. Dying he accepts. But not dying in front of spectators under bright lights. Death is the most private of all the acts that man can accomplish during his earthly life. There are natural acts, less important than death, for example lovemaking, which men cannot carry out without modesty, with curtains drawn and doors locked. The modesty surrounding death is even greater. And at this particular moment the monk is aware that dying in front of strangers, in a vast public place, brings terrible shame. And great suffering. Especially for a monk. For a monk has a sense of shame in all his natural acts. Due to modesty, a monk will not even eat a piece of fruit in public. He always eats alone. Or in the company of his brothers. This evening it will not be a matter of eating but of dying in public. Like Christ, who also endured crucifixion and His death agony in public. Like heinous criminals, who are also executed in public before a crowd of people ...

"Father, pray for me too, because I can no longer pray. I'm terribly afraid."

They're traveling in the country now. There are no lights anywhere. There is not even a village to be seen. It is very dark.

Suddenly the car leaves the road, and drives over a field. They feel the thick grass, soft as a cushion, under the wheels. They even notice the fragrance of the earth, and the scent of the vegetation, trampled by the wheels of the car. And when their eyes have grown accustomed to the darkness, they see another car, with bright, blinding headlights, speeding towards them. It is a small van. Like those used in prisons. The interior is lit up. There are two men inside. Both in uniform. And there are wooden benches. The van stops suddenly a few centimeters from the prisoners' car, crushing the grass of the field. One of the men gets out of the van, leaving the door open. He shouts to the two men in civilian dress, "Damn it, you realize you're more than an hour late? What in the hell happened on the way?"

He is coarse, furious, insolent. He looks to see if the two prisoners are in the car and yells to them to get out. The monk and Sabina try again to open the door, without managing it.

"Dirty dogs!" the man in the van shouts. He opens the doors and pulls Sabina out like a piece of rubbish. Then the priest. Shouting to them, "Out, dirty dogs, out! Get into the van. And fast!"

With all his strength he shoves Father Akathist into the van. The monk gets caught in his cassock and falls as he climbs in. Before he gets up Sabina is also pushed into the van, which is already moving. The trip only lasted for two or three minutes, and the car came to a stop. Before them was a flight of steps. When they were pushed out, the prisoners saw, for the first time in their lives, an airplane.

"Up the steps fast, faster, faster..."

A few moments later Father Theophorus Akathist and his sister-in-law Sabina were in the airplane. They were met at the door by a hostess. She too was furious. Because they had been waiting for them a long time.

With the engine running. They had been ordered to wait for them. Not to take off without them. And now they were angry at them. Everyone looked at the latecomers with hatred. The hostess showed the monk and Sabina to two seats. They were the only ones that were not taken. The others were all occupied, by all sorts of people. Soldiers, women, and a lot of children. As soon as Sabina and the monk were seated and had their seat belts fastened, the plane took off. The moment the plane left the ground, Sabina's head fell backward. Her body became soft. Like a dress. She had fainted. She could not go on. She was exactly like her white horse, the day she was returning from the city, with her father's coffin. The horse that had stopped in the middle of waters that were flowing too fast beneath him. The horse became dizzy. And without the help of Nicholas, who had gone into the water and covered his eyes while leading him to the far bank, the horse would have fallen down. Sabina had also become dizzy. Events were following each other too fast, too unexpected, too distressing. She could not live in the middle of the torrent. She was overcome with malaise. Like her white horse in the middle of the rising waters which flowed with greater and greater force, more and more threatening.

"Is the lady sick?" the hostess asked, offering her some candy, and getting no response from Sabina. She brought her some water. A pilot in uniform left the cabin and approaching Father Akathist told him, "During this entire trip, neither you nor the lady will speak to anyone at all. Do you understand? Not a word. To anyone."

"I understand," the monk replied.

"Not even to the hostess. If you have something to say, let me know. I'll be in the cabin, beside the pilot.... I hope I have made myself clear."

"Yes," the monk answered.

And irresistibly driven by a force he did not recognize, and, out of character, he dared to ask, "Where are they taking us?"

"To Frankfort am Main," the pilot said. And he left.

Sabina drank the lemonade she was given. She hadn't eaten all day long. As she was drinking her glass of lemonade, Father Theophorus thought about the name Frankfort am Main. This name was fixed in his head as though imprinted in letters of fire. He knew nothing, or next to nothing, about Franfort am Main. He thought it must be a city in Germany. It was definitely the name of a city. That's all he could remember about this name. In the seminary at the Vrancea monastery, the novices learned how they should act to win paradise. Father Akathist was a very good seminarian. He knew all the lives of the saints, the *Apophtegms* of the Fathers. He knew the *Psalterion* by heart, the celestial hierarchies, and the terrible tactics the monk must use in his struggles.... Of geography, history, and all the other subjects pertaining to this world, the monk Theophorus is ignorant. For a monk is a person who has definitively left the earthly Jerusalem and is on the way to the heavenly Jerusalem. Of course, he hasn't gotten to heaven yet. That is certain. But he is not less certain that he has left the earth. For this reason, the monk has no interest in learning about earthly things and a world he is no longer a part of...

Suddenly the priest realizes that even if he knew all that a man could know about Frankfort am Main, that would not be of any use to him. How would it help him to know, at this time, how many kilometers away Frankfort am Main is, the number of its inhabitants, how big it is. To know about its resources, its past, its finances? That would be of no use to him. That would be pointless information. Like all secular fields of knowledge which teach you what things are like and how many of them there are, but which never answer the questions "why?" and "to what purpose?". The monk, even if he had learned all this, would not be any further ahead. He did not know why they had taken him out of prison, why they had dressed him and Sabina in the spoils of martyrs, and why they had put them on this plane to take them to Frankfort. That in particular is the essential.

The other passengers doze, read, smoke, drink something, or talk among themselves.

"Would you like something else to drink?" the hostess asks Sabina.

"Another glass of water, please."

"And you, Reverend?"

"Nothing. Today is a fast day. The feast of the Beheading of St. John the Baptist."

"As you like," the hostess says, ironically.

"Why are we on this plane, Father? Where are they taking us now?"

"To Frankfort am Main," Father Theophorus replies.

"What is Frankfort am Main?"

"A town. In Germany, I think. But I'm not sure..."

"And why are they taking us there?"

"I don't know. Only God knows. And the militia."

There are no militiamen near them, because no one can escape from the plane. It is a flying prison. A plane with the initials PRR, the Penitentiary Republic of Romania.

IX

The Sun Sets in the West

THE AIRPLANE IN WHICH THE MONK
priest Theophorus and his sister-in-law are
confined took off an hour ago. It's flying toward
the west. It should arrive at Frankfort am Main before
midnight.

It is August 29, 1964, late in the evening. A few
kilometers away from the airport where the prisoners'
plane will land, there is a glass and concrete building
where an office of the American military intelligence
in Europe is located. It is built, like all US Army quarters, at the edge of the woods, in the middle of the
countryside. Far from any residence. Like all the US
government buildings in Europe, it is immeasurably sad,
aseptic. Like a desert with electricity. One would call it
the architectural image of a desert. It is the desert itself
made out of glass and concrete. The people who live
and work in the geometric offices with linoleum, neon
lights, and plastic are far from themselves, and from
other men. Just like in the desert. A desert where man
not only does not encounter anyone else, but where
he does not encounter himself. Man has abandoned
his person, his self, to become an American and a
bureaucrat. That is to say, in order to become incorporated into an office like that of the American military
intelligence at Frankfort am Main, like being filed in
the appropriate place. The tragedy of the civilization
of the USA is that they go about things like a great
sculptor, who, because he has created masterpieces out
of granite and marble, insists on shaping water with
the same tools he has used to chisel and fashion stone.

He refuses, out of pride, to understand that while he has really produced magnificent works in marble, he will never be able to cut and mold water. Americans apply to matters of the spirit the same techniques, the same tools, and the same methods which they have used to build a formidable material civilization. They make just one mistake: they treat the things of the spirit like they deal with banking, industrial and business matters. And that's the same as wanting to shape water with a hammer and chisel, under the pretext that these instruments have been tried out and tested on granite... David Lincoln Goldwin, colonel in the US defense intelligence in Europe, is one of these men. He is now in his aseptic office near the airport. In front of Colonel Goldwin sits the poet Ovid Panteleimon, dressed in new clothes, shaved, with a good haircut. Professor Ovid Panteleimon has been in the West for four days. He escaped after the murder of the miller Nicholas Akathist. He had neither a closet nor a mill to hide in. And for that reason, his escape to the West succeeded. For, to succeed in an exceptional situation, one finds himself necessarily in the position of a man with his head under water. He has to come up so he can breathe. He has to emerge from the water. The status quo is death. When he got to the West, to Austria, the free country which is closest to Romania, the poet Ovid Panteleimon was arrested and sent to the American counterespionage agency. It is the American military intelligence that receives all the refugees from the East. They treat fugitives in these special offices in the Federal Republic of Germany exactly like one treats a chemical substance in the course of a laboratory analysis. They think that this way they can find out if the refugees are really people who could no longer breathe in the Penitentiary Republics, like men with their heads under water, or if they are agents sent by the Muscovites. The result of this work, because it is exclusively mechanical, like a chemical analysis, is that all the true Muscovite spies pass the test, and the majority of the unfortunates are forced back to the land of the Muscovites or one of their Penitentiary Republics on the eastern outskirts of Europe. With Professor Ovid Panteleimon, the process was quicker. He was known for his writings, translated into all the languages of the West. He was known because he had been a minister and the greatest poet of the Condottiera and of Romania. For four days and four nights Ovid Panteleimon has been in custody in the offices of the military intelligence and does not have the right to talk to anyone except US counterintelligence agents who are stupidly bent on photographing the soul, feelings, and dreams of the brilliant poet, just as one takes pictures of material objects. From the moment they had photographed the moon, they told themselves, with the pride of genius technicians, why wouldn't they manage to photograph the soul of man, his religious sentiments, his metaphysical concerns, and his dreams?

This evening of August 29, while the poet Ovid Panteleimon was reading from the Bible that the Americans have given him along with clothing, cigarettes, chocolate, and chewing gum, the passage from the Gospel that will be chanted the next day, August 30, at the service for the tenth Sunday after Pentecost, where it is written, "Amen, amen I say to you, if you have faith the size of a mustard seed, you will be able to say to this mountain, 'move from here to there' and it will move. Nothing will be impossible for you." They called him to the office of Colonel Goldwin.

"Professor, you have told us the most tremendous story we have heard since the Second World War, twenty years ago.... Your story is terrible. Poignant. You have escaped from the Penitentiary Republic of Romania. Here you are, in the free world. You are even rich. Very rich. Because your wealth is imminent. Your account, the adventures you had during your escape, will bring you an amount..."

"You have already calculated the number of copies to be printed of the book which I haven't even written yet, and you already know how much I'll make.... With your electronic instruments that calculate how many grains of sand there are on the moon, that doesn't surprise me. But in spite of the awe and boundless admiration I have for you, I tell you again, Colonel, that I did not escape to save my skin. If it had been for myself alone, I would have done it long ago.... I escaped to save from death and from prison two human beings, the dearest to me on this earth, a holy monk and a woman, his sister-in-law, who have been hatefully accused of a horrible murder. In a few days, tomorrow or Tuesday, they will be tried. It's on their account that I escaped.... By traveling under the train cars, hanging on like a fifteen-year-old kid, me, an old man..."

"Just because of that your story will be unbelievably successful. We have it all figured out. The altruistic angle is the main element. You, a man over sixty years old, risked your life, faced incredible danger, crossing mined fields, getting through barbed wire.... Suffering from hunger and thirst for fifty-four hours. Hanging onto a train car. At your age. It's amazing. You people from East Europe astonish us with your resources, your tenacity, endurance, inventiveness.... Your life is incredible. You, a great poet, university professor, editor of journals, former minister, lived in a closet for twenty years, under the nose of the police, right in the center of Bucharest, under foreign occupation.... This is a performance without precedent. It's a championship. You have broken all the records.... You are greater than Monte Cristo, in your closet..."

"Is that all you have retained from my story, Colonel?" asks the professor.

"I have kept the essential. You have broken the world record for resistance to the occupier and invader of your country. It's a record that will be recognized in the history of our times."

"It's not a matter of a championship, Colonel. I did not escape to break the record held by Monte Cristo, or to write a bestseller, but to save the lives of two human beings, a saint and a woman who are in terrible danger of death. They did not commit the crime they are accused of. And for which they will be killed. I beg you to grasp what I'm saying.... I will soon be before the supreme tribunal and will not be asked if I have broken the record for physical endurance by spending twenty years in a closet, or by crossing borders, like a professional gangster, or if I have huge numbers of books printed...

"No, Colonel. I will be asked if I have done everything possible, after arriving here, to convince you to save the lives of the monk and the woman who will be killed, in several days or several hours, for a crime they did not commit. I was a witness, from inside the mill, that they were not the killers. I saw with my own eyes how and by whom the miller Nicholas Akathist was killed, by a thrust of the knife in his back.... It is my duty as a witness that I must fulfill. It is a duty concerning the truth in heaven and on earth, a sacred obligation, to save the lives of the monk and the woman..."

"You always slip into metaphysics, the abstract, the unreal...", Colonel Goldwin says. "That's your peculiar defect. All the peoples on the vast outskirts of Eastern Europe have the fault of confusing and complicating the simplest things. You are never able to keep to the essential. To be *sachlich*, as the Germans say."

"To be *sachlich*, to keep to the essential, is precisely

to save those two beings who, starting from Monday, starting from the day after tomorrow, risk losing their lives for a murder they did not commit."

"We have confirmed your account. We are perfectly aware of its accuracy. The Romanian newspapers recount, for the first time, a crime with an abundance of details, describing how a priest monk killed his own brother, stabbing him in the back, on the National Holiday, to take his wife and to take revenge on him for making a gift of his mill to the Party of Collaborators. That is just what you have told us. We saw that in the newspapers right after your escape. We know that the monk and the woman are in danger of death. You were hidden in the mill of the Condottiera for only two months. But your description, recorded on our tape recorders, of the life of the brave peasants of Vrancea, the Akathists, your Not Seated, is poignant. You have forgotten nothing. You are still a very, very great poet, in spite of your twenty years in a closet. An existence which could have led to your physical and moral decline. Your escape confirms that physically, you're still in shape. In good shape. A champion even. And your account of the life of the Akathists, the peoples of the Penitentiary Republics of East Europe, confirms your moral condition. You have not been weakened by your twenty years of life in a closet. Spiritually, this is also a record. Our officers of the intelligence service were deeply moved as we listened to you. This is the first time that they have had, from a single witness, a complete picture of the suffering of the herd-like republics set up by the Muscovites over half the globe. The government of the United States will be even more edified. Motivated to continue the armed struggle everywhere to establish the American way of life in the world. Your story confirms for us that we must wage war everywhere, to impose our democracy... Your story will help us to use even the atomic bomb, if necessary, to promulgate American freedom over all the earth. Your story will be disseminated everywhere and given at no charge to our boys who are fighting against Muscovite ascendancy in Asia, Africa, and Latin America. Your story will make our marines even braver. They will fight doubly hard..."

"It's a matter of something else entirely, Colonel. It is absolutely necessary to save..."

"As soon as it is published, your story about the mill of the Condottiera will be a bestseller.... You will be better known than a radio or television star. You will be more famous than Kravchenko. You will be more famous than Churchill. Do you know how many copies of Churchill's memoirs have been printed?..."

"On Monday, the day after tomorrow, the lives of the innocent, the monk and the woman, will be in danger. The collaborators will begin their trial. And they will condemn them, Colonel.... They must be saved. Help me! This is the only thing that matters, not the press run, not the courage of the marines, not the incentive to use your atomic bomb.... Let us prevent two murders that will be committed, if we do nothing.... And you can do something. You are the great America, formidable."

"Take it easy, Mr. Panteleimon. We must never forget the essential. And what I have just said is the main thing. Let's go over this again, if you're willing. Because I want you to agree to what we'll decide on doing."

"You'll do something for the holy monk and the poor woman?"

"Certainly we'll do something. Yankees are always efficient. Very efficient. And they always do something when they should. So let's go back over this. All of this. From the beginning. Sunday August 23, when the Party of the Romanian Collaborators celebrates the day of the invasion and occupation of the country by the

Muscovites, an occupation which all the Romanian people are obligated to celebrate as their National Holiday, you were alone at the mill of the Condottiera, in your hiding place."

"No," the professor says. "Since I knew there was no one near the mill or in the village, because all the inhabitants without exception had to go to cry out publicly in a chorus that they are happy to have been occupied by the Muscovites and despoiled of their property, happy to have been organized in herds in the new society of sheep, happy to be reduced to the state of beasts of burden and to live in a society of the herd type, with armed guards who have the power of life and death over them.... Since I knew there was no one in the village to see me and inform on me, I left my hideout. Even when I lived in Bucharest, in the closet, I would leave to get some exercise. Each time, I was sure that there would be nobody to see me. That's why, aware that I was alone at the mill, I walked around inside the house. I looked out the window, because I didn't dare go outside, as I knew that would always be very dangerous. Around five o'clock in the afternoon, as I was looking out the window, I heard the noise of a motor. I hid behind the curtains, and saw the militia jeep. My friend, the miller Nicholas Akathist, was returning from the celebration. Dressed in new clothes, in the national costume given to him by the Party so that he could wear it the day of the public donation of the mill. Zid Caracal, who drove the jeep, got out with Nicholas. They went inside together. I hid, and saw them go in. Nicholas was tired, weary from marching in front of the platform where Mavid Zeng was. I saw them and heard them very well from my hiding place. I even heard the labored breathing of Zid Caracal, as he was quite near me. There was only a pine board partition between us. Zid Caracal, that sinister character, who had been involved in shady dealing, had been an entertainer at fairs, and a thief, and who had spent more than half his life in prison, this common criminal whom the Muscovites enthroned as master of the village of the Akathists and right arm of Mavid Zeng, refused to sit down. He looked at Nicholas, who drank two jugs of cold water.

"Zid said to Nicholas, 'Now everything is in order. You have made a gift of your mill to the Party. Posterity will no longer be able to say that the collaborators and the founders of the social order of herds have plundered the people. They will no longer be able to say that we have despoiled you, stolen from you, that we have taken your mill by force. Now there is a deed you signed, that you read at the rostrum, in public. You're happy, I hope?'

"'I am happy, Your Exalted Comradeship,' Nicholas replied. He seemed tired. He wanted to be alone. To go to bed. But he could not tell Zid Caracal to go away. The keeper can enter the stable when he wants to, and the animals do not have the right to tell him to leave.

"'You see, Nicholas, how reasonable we are. When we make a mistake, we're not ashamed to admit it and then correct it.'

"Zid Caracal opened the window. He looked outside. He continued, 'The main thing in life is not to make mistakes. It's human to make mistakes. The Party of Collaborators makes them too. It would be stupid of us to maintain the opposite. Even the Muscovites, who are so great, make mistakes. It's human. Our merit is that we rectify them. Have you ever heard about the business of the birds in China? The Party compiled statistics, and established scientifically that the birds in the sky of China, those useless beaks, were eating quite a great quantity of grains of wheat, rice, corn, and a thousand other grains, that could have fed some dozens of millions of Chinese for a whole year. To recover those millions of tons of grains, stolen by the birds, and to give them to the Chinese, the Party of Collaborators over there ordered the mobilization of the people, and the killing of all the birds that crisscrossed the sky of China. And the order was executed. In the months that followed, all the birds were exterminated. They expected an abundant harvest the next year. But that was disappointment. The birds were no longer in China to eat the grain, but three-quarters of the harvest was devoured by insects, worms, and other tiny beasts, which had saved their lives because there were no more birds to peck at them in the fields. And the tiny pests had eaten the harvest. So they noted the results of the error. They gave the order to make the survivors return, because birds carried out indispensable work for Chinese agriculture, in culling the little beasts from the fields teeming with them. The Chinese, in spite of their discipline and meticulousness, couldn't take the place of birds, as the insects were too small, almost invisible. So they granted amnesty to the birds. They ordered them to return to China as quickly as possible. We have done the same thing here. On August 23, 1944, the day when our Popular Republic was established, we exterminated and eliminated from society a huge number of people. That was for reasons of social hygiene, asepsis. You, the miller, your wife, your brother the monk, and millions of others were expelled or exterminated. Like the birds in China. Later, we concluded that you could be tremendously useful. Like the birds in China. And we granted you amnesty in 1956, and recalled you from the labor camps. Today, we have gone even further. We have made restitution for confiscated goods, while telling you to give them to the Party yourselves, as evidence of your esteem for us. That's what you've done with your mill. Didn't you find that it was a fine thing to read your letter from the podium saying that you love nothing in the world more than the Party of Collaborators and the Muscovites, and that you are giving them what is more valuable to you than anything on earth, your own mill, begging the Party to do you the honor of accepting it? Did you see that the people had tears in their eyes? Did you see how moved they were? Aren't you happy?'

"'I am very happy, Your Exalted Comradeship,' Nicholas replied. He was leaning against the wall, since he could no longer stand up, but neither did he dare to sit down, as long as the great, the all-powerful Zid Caracal was standing.

"'You're not familiar with the Party's decision in China, my poor Nicholas. It was a coup. After the amnestied birds returned to Chinese territory, they made them understand that they could only eat worms, insects, and little beasts detrimental to agriculture, and that they couldn't touch the grain, as they had before their expulsion. Grain is for the Chinese. Not for birds. You didn't know that, Nicholas?'

"'I did not know it, Your Comradeship.'

"'But you believe me when I declare that it is true?'

"'I believe you, Your Exalted Comradeship.... Of course I believe you. But I don't really understand how the Chinese party could talk to the birds and tell them to eat only harmful pests and not grain. Birds don't know how to read or to talk. How could they have found out about the Party's orders?'

"'It was due to fear. You know, Nicholas, that when someone is afraid, he has no need of reading or of understanding. When someone is afraid, he obeys. Automatically, without even being conscious of the order. Do you understand that?'

"'Yes, Your Exalted Comradeship.'

"'And you believe that the birds obeyed the order not to touch a single grain and to content themselves with just worms and insects'

"Nicholas smiled without wanting to. What Zid Caracal has just told him is too outrageous. Of course, he is obliged, like the twenty million Romanians have been for twenty years, to say what the occupiers and collaborators say, but he smiled.

"'I do believe you, Your Exalted Comradeship. But I doubt that the birds, with their animal nature, only eat worms and don't touch grain under orders from the Party. Please understand me, Your Comradeship. I'm not saying it isn't true.... Maybe the birds realized, just like men do, that an order from the Party must be scrupulously carried out, and knowing that each grain belongs to the Party of Collaborators, they must no longer touch the smallest grain with their beaks...'

"'Here you are mistaken, Nicholas. The birds did not execute the orders of the Chinese Party. They are in the same class as enemies of the Party, priests, millers, intellectuals, farm owners, businessmen, industrialists.... The same as the birds. A category that understands nothing about anything. Who cannot be salvaged. Who cannot be integrated into an organized society. It is a recognized fact that the birds of China are not a disciplined flock, that can be commanded. Like sheep, cows, and other cattle. Like children, women, and men. And since they refused to comply with the discipline of the Party and life in a herd-like society, which requires eating what you're given and only doing what you're asked, the Chinese decided to exterminate them once for all. This time, there will not be another amnesty. There will be no more birds alive in China. Chinese laborers will have eyeglasses like microscopes. They will replace the birds. And we too exterminate and kill any element that runs the risk of being undisciplined. All millers will dream about their mills. And they will never fall into line. Do you agree?'

"'I really do not know. I myself have dreamed all my

life of becoming a miller, because I was hungry. I had been hungry for ages and ages and I felt that my hunger was not just my own hunger, but that it was hereditary. And I dreamed of bread. And polenta. I dreamed of a mill. But I have only been a miller for a few months.'

"'You have been a miller for a few months. And you will dream your whole life of becoming one again. For that reason, your brother will kill you ... Because you are a noxious element. Dangerous.'

"'My brother will kill me?' Nicholas asks. 'You must be joking. My brother is a saint. He has never killed a fly. How could he kill his brother? You've got to be joking, Your Exalted Comradeship. About the birds in China, I have some doubts, and I apologize, but about my brother, I am sure that he will not kill me. Not me. Not anyone. He would give his life for no matter whom. He would not take the life of anyone, not an animal's or a man's. Ever. He is a saint.'

"'Look at him,' said Zid Caracal. 'Do you see your brother coming back?'

"Nicholas Akathist and Zid Caracal were near the window. Beside each other. They were looking toward the road. They saw the priest approach.

"'You see your brother?'

"'Of course I see him,' Nicholas replied. 'I saw that he marched in the column of consumptives, people with tuberculosis. Like all the priests. The parade of the sick is over. My brother is returning to the village. That's to be expected, isn't it?'

"'Your brother is coming to kill you. He'll take advantage of the fact that you are the only two in the village. He'll stab you in the back with a knife. See, this very one. Your knife. He'll stick it between your shoulders and you'll die. That will make things better for all of us. The village will be cleansed of you, you'll be dead. Of your brother and your wife, who will go to prison.

For fratricide and murder. The village of the Akathists will be clean.'

"'You can't be serious, Your Exalted Comradeship. I don't know what you're getting at. Why are you saying that my wife and my brother will go to jail?'

"'Because they are going to kill you. You don't believe me?'

"'I do not believe you, Your Exalted Comradeship.'

"'Come with me to ask your brother if he hasn't come to an agreement with your wife, Sabina, to kill you. You show him the knife and ask him if it is or isn't true that he got back to the village before the others in order to kill you...'

"'Of course I'll come with you.'

"Zid Caracal and Nicholas went out to meet the priest Theophorus. To ask him if it was true that he wanted to kill his brother the miller.

"In the middle of the road, in front of the mill, Nicholas stopped and said, 'Your Exalted Comradeship, it's stupid for me to ask my brother such a thing. It is a sacrilege. I know that he is a saint. It is not possible for me to ask a saint such a thing...'

"'You don't believe that he's coming to the village at this very moment, to kill you?'

"'My brother is a saint, Your Comradeship, a great saint. He does not intend to kill me.'

"'If he doesn't intend to kill you, so much the worse for him. I am obligated to do it instead.'

"As he said this, Zid Caracal stayed a little behind, and plunged the knife with all his strength into the back of the miller Nicholas Akathist, who fell dead."

"You didn't leave to get help for the victim?"

"Of course I did. Immediately after he committed the murder, Zid Caracal got into his jeep and disappeared behind the fir trees on the road going up to the Castle of the Cow. I rushed to Nicholas. His heart had stopped. I wanted to do something. To help the poor man, Nicholas Akathist, so admirable. But, behind me, on the road, two children appeared. They were Sava and Tinca Trifan, the two children in the village with scabies. I saw them go up to the body of the dead man, and listen to his heart. Then they went running up to the Castel Vaca to inform Zid Caracal of the murder. I was heartbroken. Nicholas Akathist represented for me the land of Romania, with everything most characteristic of it. He was a peasant. He had dreamed of having a mill his whole life. He had one for a few months. Then he spent fourteen years in prison, precisely because of the mill, and on August 23, 1964, twenty years later, he was killed. All because of his mill. The poor man wasn't a miller for even one year.... To suffer his whole life and die for that reason! I think that God and the Condottiera, the Mother of God, will give him a mill in heaven with a wheel that will turn round for eternity!..."

Professor Ovid Panteleimon weeps. He dries his tears. He is overwhelmed with grief. He loved the Akathist brothers who symbolized for him heaven and earth, the land of his birth.

"We have recorded all these things, from the start," says Colonel Goldwin. "It is utterly heartrending. But it's a little too hard to swallow. We don't doubt the authenticity of your story. We've been able to verify it from articles in the Romanian press. It's all true. But for us, Americans, and even for certain Europeans, for the English, French, and Belgians, this story is not believable. Because such things don't happen where we live. And man really believes just what happens to him personally or to his family. To get back to the facts, after the crime, you fled from the mill."

"I left, of course. The mill was now in the hands of the collaborators. Nicholas was no longer there to hide me. I ran toward the West. I hung onto the first train I saw, like a madman, under the cars, and I got to Vienna. The Austrian police handed me over to the Americans. And they brought me here, to Frankfurt. To your office. And here, I ask you, on my knees if necessary, you Americans who are the masters of half the world, to save the lives of these two innocent people, Father Akathist and the widow Sabina Akathist. In a few days they will be killed. Save them, I beg you. You can do it. Zid Caracal is the murderer. I saw it with my own eyes..."

"It's impossible to intervene," Colonel Goldwin says. "There is only one way for you to present your testimony. That is to return to Romania and have Zid Caracal take down your statement, the one who is in charge of the investigation and is at the same time the murderer. But that is clearly not advisable."

"There are the UN, the League of Human Rights, Interpol, the International Court of Justice...so many international institutions..."

"No international institution has the right to interfere in the internal affairs of a country. Murder is an internal matter. Every country is free to condemn, execute, or free a murderer. Or murderers. Every law concerning crime is national. There are no international laws. If some Englishmen, for example, feel like throwing five hundred people into the Thames one night, and if they want to let the murderers go unpunished, that's totally legal. No one has the right to meddle. Murder, assassination, and theft are national matters. Each state is sovereign. We Americans as exploiters of the oil in Saudi Arabia are obligated to watch how the Saudi police cut off the hand of a kid for stealing a fig. That is their law. We only have the right to give an injection to the unfortunate boy before they cut off his hand. So he'll suffer less. And we only obtained this right after years and years of negotiations. We cannot prevent the Romanians from putting your friends to death for a murder they didn't commit. Such is the situation. *Dura lex sed lex.* They will not be the only innocent people unjustly convicted. Nor, unfortunately, the last..."

"I beg you, save them!"

"We can only promise what we can manage to do. It is true that we can do a lot. We are the masters of the world. It's true. And we're pragmatic. Practical. *Sachlich.* Even in religious and metaphysical matters we are realistic and practical men. In our country a church is as rich and quite as well organized as a bank. Or a business dealing in beans. And to give you a proof of our humanity and our pragmatism, as we have both these characteristics, being both sentimental and materialistic, here's what we have done for you and your friends."

Colonel Goldwin picks up the phone and asks that Mr. Oppenheimer be shown in. He is a civilian, and exactly like other American businessmen.

"Professor, Mr. Oppenheimer is the president of the Free Committee. I want to make clear that it is a private organization in the United States. It has nothing to do with the administration or government."

Professor Ovid Panteleimon rises and answers Mr. Oppenheimer's "How do you do."

"The Free Committee is a powerful organization," Colonel Goldwin says. "And very rich. It is more effective than the government because it is private. It is rich because in the US charitable donations are tax-exempt. And in contributing to charity, the great bankers do good business. Mr. Oppenheimer and the Free Committee are in charge of the matter of concern to you. Two years ago now, they reached an agreement with the government of the Romanian Republic, according to which, for a sum of ten thousand dollars, paid in cash to an agent of the PRR, your country frees every person requested by the Free Committee within forty-eight hours. The delivery of persons ordered by the Free Committee and the payment for them in dollars are carried out here, at the Frankfort am Main airport. Their representative pays with one hand and receives the parcel with the other..."

"What parcel?"

"The person ordered by the Free Committee, whom the agents of the PRR hand over to us! Up to the present we have purchased thousands of people. The Penitentiary Republics of Eastern Europe have a terrific need for currency. They've seen that we buy men, women, and children in large quantities, always for cash, and they're very conscientious about their deliveries. They dress them in new clothes before shipping them. Packaging counts for a lot, as in any business. At the present time the PRR gets more currency through the sale of men than from all the other items they export. They make fabulous amounts each year by exporting living human merchandise. At the beginning, they delivered a man for twenty thousand dollars. That was extremely expensive. Most of the buyers were families in America. A family there could buy their son, mother, brother, or father. It was a sentimental matter. And sentiments cost dear. Since the Free Committee took the business in hand, the price of a man has been reduced by half. They don't pay more than ten thousand dollars a head. That suits the Romanians, because now it's not a small operation any more, an occasional transaction, as it was before. Now it's a big business. A supermarket. The Romanian government receives ten thousand dollars. Five million French francs. And what do they deliver to us in exchange? A man, a woman, or an old man who, over there in their country, has no value and produces nothing. Worse than that. Usually it's an unproductive man who is rotting away in a prison.

When they sell him to us, they make ten thousand dollars. That's how we teach them that human life has a price. A great price. And each human life is worth its price, in dollars, since each time they hand over a fine specimen of a human being, they receive payment in a strong currency in exchange. In cash. In good dollars. Our theologians have congratulated us, telling us this is the way to make the Muscovites understand that the human person has value. And even a value in dollars.... And they will end up by no longer treating men like beasts. And killing them. They will be more careful with human life."

"They will be sparing of human life because they know they can sell it abroad," Professor Ovid Panteleimon says. He is deeply disturbed. For twenty years the Party of the Collaborators and the Muscovite occupiers have despoiled the Romanian people of all their goods. They grouped them together in a herd, beat them, and made them work, exactly like animals are treated. Because with beasts, you take their milk, you shear them and take their wool, you take their young, you mate them when you like, and you pasture them at will. Then when they are no longer serviceable and productive, you kill them. And now the professor learns that the collaborators with the occupiers not only kill men like animals, after treating them as such during their whole existence, but they also sell them abroad, like cattle is sold. They sell men, in 1964, right in the middle of Europe. Under the eyes of the whole world. For ten thousand dollars a head. A set price.

"They sell men like they sell animals. They export human flesh for dollars, abroad."

Professor Ovid Panteleimon weeps. With big tears. Like a child.

"You are needlessly complicating things, Professor," Colonel Goldwin says. "You have to be pragmatic."

"They are selling men to you. And you give them dollars. Dollars they use to become more powerful. Dollars they use to buy arms. To better guard the prisoners in the Penitentiary Republic of Romania."

"You're mistaken, Professor. They do not buy more weapons with the dollars we give them. They see we are fair in doing business and that we buy more and more prisoners, and they have become confident. With the dollars they receive from us, they buy, always from us, beauty products for their wives, American cars, home appliances, clothing.... They have built forbidden cities in Romania, forbidden towns where only the rulers of the country live, in luxury and opulence that no American multimillionaire could indulge in. Of course, the people don't have the right to enter these forbidden towns, the towns of the PC. Just as in *A Thousand and One Nights*. All around them are minefields, barbed wire, moats. So that the people will not see the fabulous luxury the collaborators live in, and will not stone them. There are dozens and dozens of forbidden towns in Romania. That's what they do with our money. This way, the ten thousand dollars that we pay for each man come back into our pockets with profit. We have bought your monk and the wife of your miller. They will be here before midnight, at the Frankfort am Main airport. Don't trouble to thank us. In doing good, we also do very good business. Are you happy?"

"I don't know anything any more," the professor says. "They have been sold like animals.... I cannot be happy."

"You're not living in the real world. You still have a lot to learn. You haven't yet been reintegrated into history. Into reality. One can see from a distance that you have left a life in a closet. Speaking of the closet, an American television station, which sent you an exclusive contract yesterday, has reconstructed a closet identical to the one you lived in for twenty years. They sent reporters to Bucharest. And they reconstructed it according to what they saw on the scene, and following your recorded statements to us.... This way they'll present you with your closet on television, like the one you lived in for twenty years. They're going to make the whole story come alive. Authentically, since we love realism. And truth. And documents. And then, you'll be a star for the viewers.... You deserve it, Professor. You are a champion.... Just think, twenty years in a closet! That's something unimaginable! Unique! Greater than Monte Cristo. At the same time, I'm happy because you'll see once again the persons you put in an order for. I'm talking about the monk and the lady. You'll be taken to the airport to greet them. It's better for them to be welcomed by a familiar face.... The poor people! But they'll be happy.... Like us..."

Ovid Panteleimon hides his face in his hands and prays, "Condottiera, Mother of God and of immortal souls, why have you kept me alive for twenty years in that closet, if you had only terrible things to unveil to me? Why didn't you rather let me die there?"

And the Mother of God tells Ovid Panteleimon, "You are my poet. You are the poet of the Condottiera. The poet of your people. You are the poet of all the Not Seated, of all the Akathists of the world. I kept you alive for twenty years and caused you to leave your closet safe and sound so that you could say, like the servant of Job, 'I alone have escaped to give witness to what I have seen.' And so that thanks to your witness, men who are so proud of their progress might know exactly what they were like in the year 1964."

∽⌒⌒⌒⌒∾

In the village of the Akathists, the river flows, parallel to the road. The road leads to the mill. The blades of the mill are turning. The deaf-mute woman is still

mute and deaf. The children with scabies no longer
have it. Or maybe they do. There are forms of scabies
one is not aware of. Like the absence of God. But, just
the same, people have scabies.

Mavid Zeng still comes to the village. Odor of death,
blood, and tears. Odor of decay, of flaying, of crime,
of murder.

The blades of the mill turn.

And above, the gaze of Maria Panagia, Maria Theotokos, Maria la Condottiera, the Mother of all the
Not Seated.

GLOSSARY

Acoemetic. One of the Acoemetae, Eastern Christian ascetics known for their long vigils.

Akathist. A hymn to Mary, literally meaning, in Greek, Unseated, referring to the posture assumed by the faithful in chanting it. Gheorghiu uses the term, by extension, to refer to the downtrodden people of Romania (and in the whole world) who do not have the luxury of sitting down, due to the manual labor they perform. It is in addition the last name of the two brothers in the novel, and of the village they live in.

Anterion. Cassock.

Antidoron. Blessed, but not consecrated, bread distributed at the end of Orthodox and Byzantine Catholic liturgies.

Apatheia. Control of the natural desires and emotions of the body and mortification of evil tendencies.

Apophtegms. Sayings of the Church Fathers, various collections of stories describing the practices of early Christian hermits and their advice to younger monks and visitors.

Apocatastasis. Restoration of a renewed creation at the end of the world, along with the resurrection of the dead.

Axion Estin. Hymn to Mary: "It is truly meet and right to praise you, O Theotokos, ever blessed and most pure Mother of God, more honorable than the Cherubim, and beyond compare more glorious than the Seraphim, who without corruption gave birth to God the Word, truly the Mother of God, we magnify you."

Cheirotonia. Laying on of hands in the ordination of a priest or deacon.

Christ Pantocrator. An icon of Christ depicting Him as almighty, all powerful (the meaning of the Greek word), usually placed in the dome of an Orthodox church.

Christiac. Servant of the priest, responsible assisting in the chanting at the liturgy and other duties, including burying the dead.

Coliva. A sweet pudding based on boiled wheat and served at Romanian Orthodox funeral meals, and in other Orthodox and Byzantine Catholic Churches.

Condottiera. Feminine of the Italian *condottiere*, a leader or guide, who shows the way. Applied to Mary, referring to her role in the lives of Christians. See *Hodegetria.*

Dura lex sed lex. Latin for "It is a harsh law, but it is the law."

Epitrachelion. A liturgical vestment corresponding to the Western stole.

Foehn. A dry, warm wind blowing down the side of a mountain.

Gerontikon. Collection of anecdotes and sayings of ancient hermits and monastic fathers.

Hegumen. Head of an Orthodox monastery that is subordinated to another monastery.

Hermeneia. Manuals with rules which iconographers must strictly observe.

Hodegetria. An icon of Mary showing her holding the Child Jesus and pointing to Him, the Way. The meaning of the Greek is: the one who shows the way, la Condottiera.

John Nepomucene (c. 1340–1393). Martyred by King Wenceslaus IV of Bohemia for his resistance to the king's illegal efforts to take over Church revenues belonging to an abbey. According to another tradition, disputed by many historians, John was killed because he would not reveal confidences made by the queen in confession. In any event, a popular image of John shows his head surrounded by five stars, representing the letters of "tacui," "I kept silent," referring to this second account. John was canonized in 1729.

Kravchenko. Viktor Andreevich Kravchenko, an official in the Communist party in the Soviet Union who defected to the US during World War Two. His memoir, *I Chose Freedom*, published in 1946, was a bestseller.

Maphorion. Garment covering head and shoulders.

Monte Cristo. In *The Count of Monte Cristo*, a novel by Alexandre Dumas published in 1844, the protagonist is unjustly condemned to prison, where he spends six years in solitary confinement. After an additional eight years of imprisonment, he escapes in a dramatic fashion.

Orthros. In Eastern Orthodox liturgies, the last of the night offices, the others being vespers, compline, and the midnight office.

Panagia. A title of Mary meaning all holy.

Phanar. The Greek quarter of Constantinople, after the Turks conquered the city. Phanariots were Greek officials assisting in the administration of the Ottoman empire. They had great influence in the Balkans in the eighteenth century.

Prosphora. Plural of *prosphoron.* In the Orthodox Christian and Byzantine Catholic divine liturgy, leavened bread offered and transformed into the Body of Christ.

Psalterion. The Psalter, the 150 psalms of the Bible, an important part of the liturgy and offices of prayer.

Rasophore. The first degree of monastic life, not involving formal vows.

Sachlich. A German word meaning factual, with connotations of objective, down to earth, matter of fact.

Satrap. A subordinate or local leader.

Seraglio. Here, the palace of a sultan (and not, as it sometimes means, the quarters of a harem).

Theotokos. God-bearer, Mother of God.

Trapeza. The refectory, in Eastern Orthodox monasteries.

Unsere tägliche Brot. German for "our daily bread."

Vrancea. A county in Romania, for the most part in the Moldovan region of Romania. It comprises the southern end of the eastern slope of the Carpathian Mountains, hilly regions, and lowlands.

AFTERWORD

PUBLISHED IN 1967, THE SAME YEAR as *La Tunique de peau* (*The Tunic of Flesh*), *La Condottiera* represents a turning point in the work of Virgil Gheorghiu. For it was the first of his books that he wrote directly in French. In May 1963 he was ordained a priest in the Romanian Orthodox church in Paris, on Jean de Beauvais Street, where there is now a statue in a semi-écorché[1] style of the Romanian national poet Mihai Eminescu[2]. Fifteen years after entering France illegally with his wife, crossing the French-German border at Bitche on foot, thanks to an obliging policeman who turned a blind eye to their entry, Gheorghiu saw the fulfillment of more than a dream in France: he fulfilled his vocation. Son and grandson of priests, he hadn't been able to enter the seminary in Romania, his family being without the resources to pay for his expenses. He completed his education at the military school in Kishinev (Chișinău). In June 1966, the Holy Synod of Bucharest and the Patriarch Justinian of Romania granted Gheorghiu the dignity of stavrophore oeconomus, the highest distinction that can be accorded to a married priest, in which he saw not only an ecclesiastical honor, but recognition of his literary activity.

When Gheorghiu was ordained, inspired by his faith, he believed that he had received his "tongue of fire"

---

1   An *écorché* sculpture shows the muscles without skin.
2   Mihai Eminescu (1850–1889), a Romanian Romantic poet, novelist, and journalist. He is considered to be the greatest Romanian poet, not only because of his original use of language, enriched by words from all parts of Romania and striking metaphors, but also because he took to heart the situations of all Romanians in all regions of the country.

just as the Apostles on Pentecost "were filled with the Holy Spirit, and began to speak in other tongues as the Spirit prompted them" (Acts 2:4). This allowed him to express himself directly in French, at last. Until then, he had written all his books in Romanian, his collections of poetry, his war reportage, and his first novel, *Ultima oră* (*Last Hour*), and also all his books published in France since his exile there in 1948. The first of these, *La Vingt-cinquième heure* (*The Twenty-Fifth Hour*), was translated into French by Monica Lovinescu under the name of Monique Saint-Côme. Fourteen subsequent books were translated into French by Livia Lamoure, to whom he would dedicate one of his most powerful books, *Les Sacrifiés du Danube* (*The Sacrificed People of the Danube*, 1957). Gheorghiu made the choice to write in French like his compatriots Cioran[3] and Ionesco[4], but especially like the older Panait Istrati.[5] In every adopted language there is a tentative correctness, an outmoded charm, enriched by the transfusion of the mother tongue. This makes Gheorghiu's unmistakable style even more poignant.

At his death, June 22, 1992, the obituaries, written by small-minded critics, did not do justice to their subject. They limited Virgil Gheorghiu's work to *The*

---

3   Emil Cioran (1911–1995), a philosopher whose work is characterized by pessimism, a tragic sense of history, and contemplation of the end of civilization. Living in Paris from 1937 until his death, he wrote in French from 1945 on.

4   Eugène Ionesco (born Eugen Ionescu, 1909–1994), a playwright who contributed to the theater of the absurd. After spending most of his childhood in France, he returned there permanently after the outbreak of World War II. He was elected to the Académie française in 1970.

5   Panait Istrati (1884–1935), a writer, widely traveled, whose tumultuous life is reflected in his fiction. He wrote his most important works in French, and has been called the Gorky of the Balkans.

Twenty-Fifth Hour and to their mistaken ideas about his detective novels, which they had quite probably never bothered to read. This rash judgment seemed to come from a regurgitation of previous critiques rather than from their own analysis. This would amount to considering Kafka's *The Trial*[6] as an example of court reporting, or Dino Buzzati's *The Tartar Steppe*[7] as a treatise on siege warfare. These inept critics missed the true scope of a novel like *La Condottiera*, just as they would undoubtedly have overlooked some of Graham Greene's works, in which they would probably have seen only spy novels...

Though *La Condottiera* begins as a murder mystery, the true subject of the book is the human condition in a people's republic, in this case The People's Republic or the Penitentiary Republic of Romania. On August 23, 1964, the national holiday — which, on account of the sadism proper to all totalitarian regimes, is for the oppressed population an obligatory celebration of the anniversary of the invasion of the "Muscovite" troops — the miller Nicholas Acathist is murdered in front of his mill. Almost immediately his brother, a monk, is arrested. Unlike Gheorghiu's *La Seconde Chance* (*Second Chance*, 1952) in which the brothers Boris and Angelo Podnar represent Cain and Abel, Good and

---

6   One of the best-known novels of Franz Kafka (1883–1924). Combining elements of fantasy and realism, it recounts the arrest and prosecution of Josef K., who never learns the nature of the charges against him. The surreal nature of his experiences can be seen as a commentary on the impersonal nature of bureaucracy.
7   Dino Buzzati (1906–1972) wrote novels, short stories, poetry, and plays characterized by fantasy, science fiction, and themes of alienation. *The Tartar Steppe*, his most famous work, relates the life of a young officer who spends his life guarding an insignificant border fortress. When the Tartars arrive at long last, the officer becomes ill, is dismissed, and dies before he gets home, an example of the futility of existence.

Evil, the Acathist brothers, for their part, stand for the twofold dimension of human nature. They are the incarnation of the dualism between heaven and earth, without this difference being irreconcilable. As in Graham Greene's most characteristic books, *La Condottiera* reveals its profoundly spiritual inspiration throughout the course of a detective story full of adventures. It untiringly opposes the relentless ferocity of the communist regime and the total dehumanization of Western civilization with the message of the Gospel.

In his account *Le Peuple des Immortels* (*The People of the Immortals*, 1955), where he puts fiction and recent history aside, Gheorghiu goes back to the roots of his people. For the Immortals are the Dacians, the ancestors of Romanians, whom Homer declared the most just men on earth, and of whom Herodotus said, "They believe they are immortal and neither they nor their most distant descendants will die." Here Gheorghiu celebrates the half-historical, half-mythological Zamolxis, mystical figure from among the Dacians, who "fought during their entire earthly existence . . . in order not to lose eternity." With this story, Gheorghiu seems to have foreshadowed a cycle of his novels, the Romanian tetralogy consisting of *La Maison de Petrodava* (*The House in Petrodava*, 1961), *Les Immortels d'Agapia* (*The Immortals of Agapia*, 1964), *Le Meurtre de Kyralessa* (*The Murder of Kyralessa*, 1966), and *La Condottiera* (1967). Each book is set in a Romanian village, and whether it be Petrodava, Agapia, Kyralessa, or Vrancea, it is always an incarnation of the author's village, located in the "suburbs of Europe". The county of Neamț in the Carpathians, where the action of several of his books takes place, is for Gheorghiu what Yoknapatawpha County was for Faulkner, archetype as well as idealization of the land of his birth, from which he was uprooted by his exile, as he acknowledges, "Separated from my people by exile, I continually seek them."

In *La Condottiera*, the names of characters and places have meaning, for example the Castel Vaca (Castle of the Cow), which besides obviously bringing to mind the castle to which the surveyor K. struggles unsuccessfully to gain access in Kafka's *The Castle*, recalls the Castle of the Bull, the odd name of the little school in Petricani which the young Virgil attended. As for the surname Acathist, it refers to "the most beautiful hymn, ... the most beautiful prayer of the Church [which] is named Acathist because the people chant it while standing," as well as to the inhabitants of the village of Vrancea, "the Always Standing, because it is made up solely of people without land, of dayworkers [who] are people who spend their whole existence standing, ready to sign up with an employer and follow him." To be forever standing, adds Gheorghiu, "is the position proper to the poor", which recalls their humility, the simplicity of their condition, and their dignity, inherited from the Dacians. In the character of Ovid Panteleimon, Romania's "national poet", one is tempted to discern, some major reservations aside, the tutelary figure of Tudor Arghezi[8], who died the year *La Condottiera* was published. Gheorghiu felt for this poet, who had been for a time a monk in Cernica, Romania, great admiration and gratitude. Arghezi had published Gheorghiu's early articles in his journal *Bilete de Papagal*, written the preface to his World War II chronicle *Ard Malurile Nistrului* (*The Banks of the Dniester are in Flames*, 1941), and got him work as a reporter with the newspaper *Cuvantul*. The first name of the character Panteleimon renders homage to Ovid, who was exiled to Dacia. There he

---

8   Tudor Arghezi (1880–1967), a major poet of the twentieth century, combined traditional styles and symbolism, lyricism and grotesque images of decay. He also published essays on various aspects of politics, with views ranging from leftist to monarchist.

composed his *Tristia*[9], an episode which would inspire another masterpiece of Romanian literature written in exile, *Dieu est né en exil* (*God Was Born in Exile*) by Vintilă Horia, that was awarded the Goncourt Prize in 1960, and on account of which protests were made.[10] The surname Panteleimon, which etymologically means "merciful to all", undoubtedly refers to St. Pantaleon of Nicodemia, court physician to the emperor Maximian, beheaded for his faith, and included in the most ancient martyrologies. In the universe of Gheorghiu, earth, the earth of peasants, and heaven, the heaven of priests, are both enriched by legends which draw from the wellsprings of poetry and folklore.

To this universe where it is possible to live as a human being, Gheorghiu opposes the Soviet regime and the American model. Without putting them on an equal footing, he nonetheless denounces their errors with the same virulence and appositeness. According to him, what they have in common is the making of man, in his complexity and uniqueness, an abstraction, in order to impose a norm, either ideological or societal. For in the middle of the cold war, there was no alternative other than these two camps, which issued attacks and counterattacks against each other,

---

9   *Sorrows* or *Lamentations*, five books of letters written in elegiac couplets giving expression to his grief at his exile, which lasted until his death, in what is now Romania.

10   Vintilă Horia (1915–1992), a writer. Sympathetic to Mussolini early on, he was posted to the Romanian embassy in Rome under King Carol. During World War II he was imprisoned for a time by the Nazis. Not wanting to return to Soviet Romania, he lived in Italy, Argentina, and Spain, where he was a university professor. He published novels and memoirs in Romanian, French, and Spanish. *Dieu est né en exil*, about the years Ovid spent in Dacia, is his most notable work. The protests against his Goncourt prize were due to allegations that he had been a member of a fascist organization in Romania.

in a duality fed by all the conflicts of the second half of the twentieth century. Thus under the Soviet yoke:

> The Muscovite invaders organize the countries they conquer in the same way they manage their herds on the steppes. They divide the conquered people into flocks, or departments, and put someone in charge of each flock. This official, like a shepherd, distributes food and clothing, and assigns living quarters. The flock of men must, in turn, offer the official all they produce, exactly as sheep must give the shepherd their milk, their wool, their lambs, their skin, their flesh...

While in the Made in USA society:

> Americans apply to matters of the spirit the same techniques, the same tools, and the same methods which they have used to build a formidable material civilization. They make just one mistake: they treat the things of the spirit like they deal with banking, industrial and business matters. And that's the same as wanting to shape water with a hammer and chisel, under the pretext that these instruments have been tried out and tested on granite...

This imposition of a norm, whatever its nature, leads to automatism. Gheorghiu and his wife had bitter experience of this. When Romania was invaded by Soviet troops on August 23, 1944, Gheorghiu, who was then cultural attaché at the Romanian embassy in Zagreb, decided not to go back to his country, opting for exile. He and his wife were arrested *automatically* by American soldiers convinced that they had laid their hands on the king and queen of Romania. Then they were *automatically* transferred to the American zone of a Germany bled white by war, separated and shunted from one prison camp to another for a year and a half before being *automatically* freed without ever having been tried or learning what charges had been leveled against them. Oppression by a technical, managerial society was denounced in an absurdist fashion by the character Traian Koruga in *The Twenty-Fifth Hour*, superbly portrayed by Serge Reggiani in the film directed by Henri Verneuil a few months before the publication of *La Condottiera*. In the face of "bureaucratic despotism", whether in a totalitarian or democratic society, there is only one refuge for man, Gheorghiu exhorts us, being anchored to the earth and lifted up by the spirit.

Thierry Gillybœuf
author of *Virgil Gheorghiu,*
l'écrivain calomnié (2017)